SARA

THE LONG ROAD TO THANKFUL

Scriptures taken from the Holy Bible, New International Version®, NIV®. Copyright © 1973, 1978, 1984, 2011 by Biblica, Inc.™ Used by permission of Zondervan. All rights reserved worldwide. www.zondervan.com The "NIV" and "New International Version" are trademarks registered in the United States Patent and Trademark Office by Biblica, Inc.™

HIS Publishing Group is a division of Human Improvement Specialists, llc. For information visit www.hispubg.com or contact publisher at info@hispubg.com

ISBN: 979-8-9912823-0-7 *paperback*
        979-8-9912823-1-4 *ebook*

HISPUBLISHING
GROUP

Division of Human Improvement Specialists, llc.
www.hispubg.com | *info@hispubg.com*

CONTENTS

DEDICATION

This book is dedicated to my husband, Kenneth, the rock in my world and blessing. Thank you for weathering the storms with me. You, above all men on earth, have stood beside me with arms of comfort and words of encouragement. You are a prince among men and my favorite person.

This book is also dedicated to my children, Cara and Kaye. I thank God every day for the gifts that you have been in my life.

I especially dedicate this book to my grandchildren Ethan, Wiley, Elizabeth, Mikayla and McKenzie. Grammy loves you. My prayer for you is that you seek the Lord and find Him. I pray that you will lean on Him when the storms of life come, because they will. I pray that you will dedicate your lives to Him and know that within His word you will find wisdom, life, and hope.

This book is also lovingly dedicated to my brother Sonny, my sister, and the memory of my brothers Tommy, and Chuck. The challenges we faced as children were many and God only knows the unique ways in which we were all affected. I pray God's blessings on the two of you that still remain and I see your lives as a testament to your determination and courage in the face of adversity.

INTRODUCTION

I spend my mornings at Panera Bread, eating a cinnamon raisin swirl bagel with honey walnut cream cheese, while drinking a cup of hazelnut coffee with lots of cream.

You wouldn't think that much happens at Panera, but you would be wrong. Within it's doors people meet daily to discuss trivia, have bible studies, and to simply get away from the confines of the four walls within their homes that are now...too quiet.

It was there this book was dreamed about, written, and prayed over. Every day, I see people walk through those doors at Panera from every walk of life you can imagine. There are people of all ages, people from all over the world, people who are in a hurry with places they have to go, people who sit and stay a while, and those who have no where else to go; those who are hungry and homeless.

I will never forget the freezing cold winter day a homeless man wandered in its doors. He stood not far from the entryway pacing back and forth, not sure whether he would be welcomed to take a seat within the warm interior, or not. As he stood there miserable from the cold wearing no coat, he looked beaten down.

I approached him and asked, "Are you hungry?" He barely looked at me as he replied, "Yes". I walked with him up to the counter and purchased some food and something hot for him to drink. As, we stood there, he felt he needed to explain to me why his need to eat was special so that it would help me to see and believe that he was worthy of my kindness. It broke my heart.

This book is written for the broken-hearted. Those souls who feel that they are unworthy of kindness and love for whatever reason. It is the story of my childhood. A childhood that was filled with abuse, abandonment, and heartbreak and how God brought me through the pain so that I found joy and peace and began to see that I was worthy of love.

I pray that if you have suffered openly or secretly, that you will find hope within these pages. I pray for you God's peace. This book is also written for the people who walk among the broken-hearted. I pray that your eyes are opened to the ones who suffer and that you can know that kindness does make a difference. I pray that your heart is moved to light the way for those in the dark.

CHAPTER 1

INNOCENT DAYS

For I know the plans I
Have for you declares the Lord, plans
To prosper you and not to harm you,
Plans to give you hope and a future.

—Jeremiah 29:11

When you are four years old, what do you know about the world except that you are a small vessel of need? When you feel hungry you cry to be fed and when hurt you cry to be comforted. You know there are tall people within your home and might call them dad and mom and not have any idea what that really means. The short people that live with you in your home, you might call by their first names and not fully understand or realize that they are your brothers or sisters.

Nothing spoken could be more true of the innocent days of my childhood under the age of five. Carefree days were spent by me unencumbered by the weighty decisions that were being made by the adults within my home and the chaos that existed in my four year old life.

What did my four year old self know about life except that it felt blissful? If danger existed I was too young to feel afraid or recognize it. My young days were innocent, and wild. At the tender age of four, I felt no worry as I spent countless days of wandering with my brother Chuck. Childhood days of play, fighting, crawling in the dirt, and making mud pies. Carefree and dangerous days, where I crossed the street alone and went everywhere like a street cat looking for something to jump on, crawl under, or eat. Days of adventure and exploration that included crawling under the house with my brother Chuck to discover no monsters hiding there but dirt, spider webs and bugs.

The truth is that this kind of free range parenting that allowed open doors and roaming by my brother and me at such a young age would come at great cost to our family, would impact us all, and almost cost my brother Chuck his life.

Both of my parents were well-educated professionals. My dad, Dr. H.D. Farthing, was a practicing physician and my mother, Kathryn Farthing, had been educated in Tennessee to become a registered nurse. The early years of their marriage were filled with happiness and love for each other, with a future whose promise seemed bright. Yet, within those same years, also came multiple miscarriages that brought them disappointment and the heartbreak of loss. In spite of this, they continued their pursuit of having children and in June, 1950, their first surviving child, a son, was born in Tennessee; promptly and proudly named after his father, Horace Dudley Farthing II. This success, this birth, brought such joy and encouragement to my parents that they became determined to bring more children into the world. Slightly more than a year later, their next child, a son was born and each successive year brought another child into the world and their home until they were the parents of five children. As the youngest and last child, I was born September 3, 1955, in Memphis, Tennessee.

Because our father also served in the military, our family moved place to place, never living anywhere for an extended period of time. Family life was chaotic with constant moves that took us to Tennessee, Georgia, back to Tennessee and then finally Oklahoma where we would remain.

Oklahoma living became chaotic too with continual moves from town to town. During these years we lived in several small Oklahoma towns, which included the communities of Healdton, Velma Alma, and Fort Supply before our father finally settled our family to live and where he would work for the remainder of his days in Vinita, Oklahoma located in the northeastern part of the state.

At some point, during the time period of my father's medical school training, and after I was born, our parents began to use and abuse drugs. For a time, this secret addiction raged on between them and was unknown by others. Eventually their desire for drugs and the need to be free of the overwhelming responsibilities required in taking care of five young children won out and they began drugging us so that they could go out without paying for someone to babysit us.

In time, the knowledge of their drug use became known and spread in the small town where we lived. After people became aware of their actions and clouded judgment my mother sought treatment for her drug use but no cure was found for the chaos in her marriage to my father. After her release from the hospital and return home, our mother's ability to provide loving care for us continued to fade and in time became nonexistent as depression and sleep helped to further aide her disappearance from life.

With our mother often asleep on the sofa, there were occasions in which my brother and I took matters into our own hands when faced with hunger. One particular day, as our mother slept on the sofa, Chuck and I went into the kitchen, hungry and searching for something to eat. My brother who was two years older than I, quickly claimed a box of cereal. I was only three or four years old at this time and had a strong will that knew no boundaries. I knew what my stomach wanted and it was cereal. In two shakes of a lamb's tail, I grabbed a knife, stabbed my brother in the arm, and claimed ownership of the cereal box for myself. Fortunately for my brother Chuck, and for me, the damage to him wasn't life ending.

Sadly this singular event didn't change the behavior of our mother but in order to be sure we were fed our father hired someone to cook for us and help out within the home.

Our father's main concern was centered on his job and the work responsibilities he had at the hospital. While his job kept our family fed and clothed, little else was provided by him in any healthy or emotional way that I can remember. In time, any attachment or feelings he had felt for our mother and us became replaced by his desire for another woman he met at the hospital.

Unaware and unable to feel any concern on the home front, the drug induced sleep of our mother rocked on.

With both of our parents separately untangled from their home responsibilities, my brother and I, continued to experience adventures inside and outside the home. Crawling under the house…no problem. Eating mud pies…sure give it a try. Wander all over the place in town…let's go! Showing the neighborhood boys my body parts… no problem. Let me repeat that….no problem. When you're a child with an innocent and pure heart that is unsoiled by the reality of dangerous situations everything seems ok. C.L.D. Club would be a perfect title for the Chuck and Sarah adventure club because we were certainly, "Children Living Dangerously".

I am not certain which town we were living in when danger found its way, knocked on the door of our young hearts, and came calling but the day and the event is emblazoned in my memory. On this day, while outside free range fearlessly roaming, an invisible force held me frozen in place on the city sidewalk as Chuck ran ahead of me into the street and was hit by a car. Police were called to the scene and with no parent to be found, I was gathered up and placed into a police car for a ride home while Chuck was loaded into an ambulance for a ride to the hospital. He would survive his injuries from the accident and after some time in the hospital, he returned home. He was alive, but never the same.

Sadly, Chuck had more physical and emotional trauma within those early years than the rest of his siblings. After having been stabbed in the arm during our fight over cereal and getting hit by a car, our parents, each unwilling to provide and care for Chuck, looked to find someone else to raise him. He was six years old and they brazenly took him and paraded him in the homes of aunts and uncles searching for someone, anyone, to take him. After these attempts by my parents to abandon him were met with rejection, Chuck remained in the home and the C.L.D. Club continued on with gusto.

Ignorance was childhood bliss and life seemed pretty grand until another battle at home ensued. Thankfully this time it didn't involve Chuck. This battle was a singular event with me as the only victim...the battle to get gum out of my hair. Though not dangerous or life threatening... it required scissors. Gum at bedtime. Who knew that this could be a problem? Certainly not me and apparently not my parents. With gum firmly embedded in my hair, the medical staff within my home made a quick decision. My father ordered that scissors be brought. With deliberate hands, he swiftly separated the gum from my hair and felt satisfied that the surgery was a success, but the patient looked frightful. With chopped up hair, a dirty body and pee stained pants, I was a sight to behold. Not that anyone really cared; not my mother, not my father, and certainly not my brothers. It was just one more headache and problem stacked behind a mountain of all the others.

In time, all of the chaos that occurred within their marriage brought with it the loss of the dreams they had of a life together and when that was gone, the loss of love for each other. Finally, infidelity ravaged any future hope for their marriage and tore apart the children left within the home. I was too young to know what was happening and had no idea that they were separately making decisions that would change my future and whole world. Perhaps it was long before the day my mother and father decided there was no hope for the marriage or the day their divorce was final, but when their marriage fell apart my mother disappeared and I never saw her again.

With my mother now gone and out of the picture, my father quickly moved his girlfriend and her two children into our home. From the start, this change didn't go well for me. I promptly peed on the sofa like an angry cat who uses the floor instead of the litter box. Needless to say, this new woman was not amused. Within a short time of her entering our home with her two children, my father decided that he wasn't done in his efforts to eliminate from his life the unwanted and unimportant. Like cleaning out a closet of clothes that no longer fit, his children were no exception and my oldest brother, at the age of eight or nine years old was sent to live with strangers. After dropping him off, our father promised him this was just a short stay and that he would come back to get him. But hatefully that day never came.

With his oldest son now out of the home, he decided to keep Tom, who was his seven year old son, and was forced to keep my six year old brother, Chuck. Unfortunately the work of removing the unwanted and unimportant was not finished. At the tender age of four there was nothing to prepare my young heart for the fact that my parent's marriage had come to an end and that neither parent would seek to keep me.

It was only after I was removed from my parent's home in Vinita and I was much older that I began to experience feelings of not being worthy of love. I began to feel like one of a litter of puppies that people decide to give away; proudly produced but in the end deemed inconvenient and unwanted.

So it was in the month of April, five months short of my fifth birthday, with tangled hair and a small suitcase, I stood outside my home in Vinita, Oklahoma, waiting for something. I didn't know what. I had experienced traveling with my mother to other places and even once had gone with her to my grandparents home but this day my mother wasn't at home and I wondered if my dad was going to take me somewhere. I didn't understand that this day my dad wasn't going anywhere with me, I was the one going. The emotional impact of this would take me years to unravel.

How as a four year old do you prepare your heart for abandonment? Where do you go in your mind to soothe a broken heart? What can you do when you cry for your mother but she doesn't come to erase your fears?

Maybe God prepares angels to hold you on their laps with warm arms that wrap around you while songs are quietly sung into your ear to soothe and comfort. But there didn't seem to be any angels present this day, until a car arrived at the house.

This symbolic hearse signaled the death of a family relationship that separated me from both of my parents and the opportunity to grow up with my brothers. There were no hugs goodbye that I remember, no tears of loss, no last embrace from my father, or regret on his face. He stood devoid of emotion and warmth as people, who were strangers to me, took my suitcase and placed it in their car along with me. On this life changing April day I have no memory of that angelic car ride or any memory of words spoken as I was taken miles and miles from my home to a new life, with new parents, to a new home that held a secret for me; the fact that they were raising one of my siblings, my very own sister.

CHAPTER 2

OUT OF THE ASHES

Though my father and mother
Forsake me, the Lord will receive me.

—Psalm 27:10

So it was in the month of April, 1960, five months short of my fifth birthday, that I was the last Farthing child to be sent out of the home and my childhood world was set ablaze. The family connection to my parents was burned to the ground, never to be the same. But…beautiful things can come out of the ashes.

You might wonder how does one find beauty within the ashes of a burned up life? Sometimes distance, time, and perspective are needed and each of these became absolutely necessary for me.

When I entered my new home I was too young to be afraid but I was confused. I had no idea or memory that I had a sister and often cried wanting my natural mother. I wondered where both of my parents were and when I was going home.

It took some time for me to understand that I was never going home. The truth was that my parents had abandoned my sister there years before and my mother was never coming though she had called once and had spoken to us on the phone. After some time, the waiting on her to come get us stopped, and I began to adjust.

The family that came to Vinita, Oklahoma and took me to raise provided so much that my natural parents chose not to provide. It was there in this new home the rest of my childhood story would be written and a beautiful foundation of a Christian life would be formed. I would learn of the comfort of motherly love, dwell and play in peaceful, beautiful, countryside surroundings with my sister, and be more than satisfied with plenty of food to fill my childhood hunger.

Though I had no memory of ever having been to this new home, photos revealed the fact that younger versions of my siblings and I had once sat upon the bar stools within its kitchen. These photos taken during happier moments showed my three brothers, my sister and me still united, celebrating birthdays, and eating cake. But again, I was so young, I had no memory of having ever been there.

From the ashes, a new life began for me. Gone forever were the dangerous days of roaming like a street cat, eating mud pies, hunger due to neglect, fighting over boxes of cereal with my brother, and gum in hair episodes. Not gone was my love for my natural mother and inconvenient episodes of wetting my pants which would continue for some time. I'm so thankful this family showed great patience with me during this time. I'm thankful that I wasn't made to feel shame or was punished.

These people, these strangers to me, into whose home I had returned, were country living folks and a strong family unit that consisted of five adults ranging in age from thirty-five to six-ty-three and one child, my sister, who was almost six years old. It was within the Pendletons' home and with this family that I'd live out the rest of my childhood.

I find it mind boggling how my parents made the first decision to abandon one of their own but it began one particular night in 1957 during the time period that our family lived in Healdton, Oklahoma. My parents, eager to have a night out asked the Pendletons to babysit my sister who was fourteen months older than me. All went well until they went to pick her up. She didn't want to go home with them and as young children will do, she cried to stay. It was there and then, they made the unbelievable decision to just leave their young daughter behind permanently. I can't imagine the mindset of any parent who'd do such a thing; people who'd allow themselves to casually move on without one of their children. But this choice, once made, made the next marital decisions for them as a couple and later choices made by them both to abandon more of their children, easily done.

Whatever their reasoning was for the decisions that were made or the social consequences that would follow, they were res-olute. There was no desire on their part of turning back no matter what it would mean for their children. Our natural parents made decisions that impacted all of us and changed the trajectories of their lives and ours forever. With reckless abandon they both did exactly what they individually wanted.

Though my sister and I were strangers to each other, we quickly became playmates and in our early years were best friends. She was beautiful with the most beautiful blue eyes and whatever she wanted to do, I was eager to do. I loved her.

With many acres of beautiful countryside to safely roam, and a new playmate to do it with, I found joy as we played together. New memories were created for me and the ashes of a former life were swept away. It was there that my tender young heart became rooted with love for these people. Family values were implanted, and an appreciation and love for God began. But sometimes life is like skating on a frozen pond. Thinking we are safe and secure, we skate upon its glassy surface feeling confident until we fall through thin ice.

CHAPTER 3

SHELTER FROM THE STORM

So do not fear,
For I am with you;
Do not be dismayed,
For I am your God.
I will strengthen you and
Help you;
I will uphold you with my
Righteous right hand.

—Isaiah 41:10

Storms in southern Oklahoma often send people seeking shelter, in the assurance it will protect them from the high winds, and possible tornadoes that are common in that part of the country. Once the storm has passed, people exit the shelter to see if any damage is done to their home or property. Though heavy rains and wind and an occasional tornado can bring destruction, most often upon exiting the shelter, those who sought refuge there find all is well. The sun begins peeking through the clouds and a rainbow appears. With relief and smiles, life continues with no damage done.

For a long time after coming to live with the Pendletons, a symbolic rainbow remained in my life reflecting a promise of hope and stability and all seemed well. Within these early years, I fell in love with this new family. I started first grade, made friends, changed schools after my fourth grade year, made more friends, and life was easy and sweet. I no longer constantly longed for my natural mother.

At first I was too young to worry what the future held in my new home. I only knew what four year old children can know. I knew when I felt hungry. I knew when I felt tired. I knew when I wanted to play and most of all I knew I wanted to feel the warmth of my new mother rocking me to sleep. I had never witnessed either of my natural parents express anger or saw discipline carried out by them due to misbehavior from my brothers or myself, and there was never a time we were verbally abused. I didn't know that within a few short years, the welcoming, kind, and soft behavior of the adults in my new family would harden. Due to the challenges of raising two young children who were not their own, or for reasons I will never know or understand, the hardened spirit that permeated the family seemed to gain momentum and brought unexpected angry shifts in their behavior.

With everything in my being I wish the speech given by E. H. Haywood, on November 16, 1862, more than one hundred years before I arrived at Wirt was true. He said, "Sticks and stones may break my bones, but words will never harm me." I SO wish that this was true. I wish that cruel hate-filled words didn't cause harm. I wish that there was nothing that could penetrate my delicate heart like poison. But wishes are just that....wishes.

The truth is that many years of my early childhood within my new home were sweet and happy. Nothing foretold of any impending pain. These rainbow years were wonderful and I felt loved. I came to love this family deeply with all of my heart. They were all the family I had or would ever have after being abandoned by my parents.

I loved the warm, wonderful, happy days and moments we shared. I loved the beauty of the countryside home, the abundance of Christmas gifts given during the holiday season, the birthday parties and beautiful clothes lovingly made for my sister and me to wear. All of these joy filled events colored and encouraged my heart with thoughts of love toward my new family and I felt secure. But this feeling of security and love, in time, began to unravel like a pulled thread on a garment as a result of physical abuse, verbal abuse, and later sexual abuse that happened within the home.

Sweet loving words were replaced with hateful words and actions that would sear into my soul like a branding iron and the thread of security loosened and began to unravel. I don't remember exactly how old I was when the moments of abuse within my new home began but early on, my sister and I were warned to never embarrass our family in public.

The truth is that physical, verbal and sexual abuse doesn't have to happen everyday for it to render its recipient devastated and in emotional ruins. With increased frequency, repeated abuse can be a destroyer of relationships and destroy a life if it is experienced over a lifetime without seeking help for the wounds.

All four of the adults, with Grandpa as the exception, to one degree or another were participants in the emotional and verbal abuse that occurred during my childhood years and continued even into adulthood.

What do you do when someone you love, adore, and view as a parent says that they are sorry they ever took you and that you have been nothing but a heartache to them? How do you recover from the painful realization that once again… you are not loved or wanted? What do you say when you are a teenager and your dad of the last eleven years says, "If your parents ever come back and want you…we are going to let you go!"

During my childhood within this home these hate-filled words and events became increasingly hard to comprehend. I couldn't fathom or understand what had happened or what I'd done to bring these painful moments about. I only knew that I loved and needed them.

Like a child with hemophilia who bleeds easily and dangerously when cut; I felt the cuts of the verbal, emotional, and physical abuse intensely that happened within the home.

In an effort to adapt I wanted to bury the hurt and pretend everything was great. For a time, that's what I did. I bandaged these wounds with actions and behaviors in order to cope. I became a chameleon, changing myself to become whatever my family wanted so that I wouldn't be abandoned again.

I was desperate to be loved and to feel loved. I told myself, don't cause any problems, make good grades, do whatever anyone ask of you. Don't feel too much, and even worse, if you have negative feelings, bury them. Comply, comply, comply, don't make any waves. But this adaptation by me still wasn't enough to prevent the verbal abuse that was readily dished out.

Wherever we went the beautiful clothes my sister and I were privileged to wear always showcased our family's well meaning generosity but unfortunately our new family forgot to clothe our broken hearts with kindness.

After the verbal abuse began, I began to feel there was something wrong with me and I began to think it was my fault. I began to believe it was impossible for anyone to love me.

When I look back now, though things were not perfect, I see that God loved me and was providing for me the very things I was too young to provide for myself. He was providing food, shelter, clothing and a home with a built in playmate. All the things I could possibly need. For this, I am eternally thankful.

CHAPTER 4

GLADYS AND RUEL

Children obey your parents in
The Lord for this is right.
Honor your mother and father
Which is the first commandment
With a promise so that it may
Go well with you and that you
May enjoy long life on the earth.

—Ephesians 6: 1-3

When I came into this new home, and was told to call these strangers by certain names, I complied but sometimes the heart makes the choice for you.

It was clear to me who my mother was. Her's was the lap that rocked me to sleep, gave me medicine when I was sick, and when I was sixteen, snuck letters to the post office for me, to a boy away at basic training that I ended up marrying the following year. I loved her with my entire being and her name was Gladys Pendleton.

Mother was born in Indian Territory, as it was then known, November 24, 1905, to Eula and Luther Maddox. Her early life was filled with poverty, adversity, and adventure. It was amazing to hear her story of arrival in the Healdton, Oklahoma area where she now lived. While still a teenager, her family had come there with everything they owned in a covered wagon.

I sat in rapt attention listening to her as she described her early childhood home; a home that didn't showcase privilege or any kind of wealth. She shared with me that when it was night-time, if they looked up at the ceiling in the living room of the home where she lived with her parents, two brothers and a sister, stars could be seen peaking through the boards there.

Every day, her mother Eula, and the children inside the home, would sit in the dark waiting until Eula saw their father walking down the road toward home, and then, only then, would the coal oil lamps be lit to provide light within the home.

She never shared how she met the man she came to marry but her married life began while she was still young. She was barely sixteen years old when she married Ruel Pendleton.

Understanding they had a nine year age difference peaked my curiosity, and I love a great mystery, so I decided to look up their marriage license. I was surprised to find she had listed her age there as eighteen.

There are so many questions I would love the answer to. Most curiously, why did she feel she had to lie about her age? The answer to this question, though intriguing, I will never know.

When I was old enough to read and begin to memorize scripture, my mother wanted me to memorize the sixth chapter of Ephesians. She felt it was important for me to understand what God wanted for me as a child within their home. It became ingrained within my soul like so many things did during my childhood.

She taught me how to crochet and taught me compassion for others. I watched her life of love and service to her family and those in need. Her example was instrumental in the formation of the decisions I would make in my own life.

From a kitchen bar stool perch, as a child and teenager, I would watch as my mother removed the rocks from a bag of pinto beans as they were sorted, and washed, to go into a pot for lunch on Sunday or as she rolled, dried, and cut into strips, dumplings made from scratch, which were then laid one by one into a pot of boiled chicken and thickened broth.

We all reaped the benefits of the food produced in that kitchen and even dogs on our property were rewarded and hungrily devoured the kitchen scraps. Like us, they only got the very best.

Hers were the hands that sewed beautiful dresses, recovered furniture, kneaded dough, and patted babies bottoms while rocking them to sleep. She spent hours and hours crocheting in the living room in the afternoons.

The closet shelf in her room was stacked high with beautiful crocheted blankets lovingly waiting for the next wedding shower of a new bride. Baby booties, tucked in boxes, waited the arrival of new little ones at Church. Busy, busy, hard working hands of love for others and me.

Everything that she did was amazing, and I could see what God's calling on her life looked like.

Of all the things mother was, she was an overcomer and survivor. She had experienced a health scare in midlife that almost took her life and was plagued by daily headaches every morning that would confine her to her bed until the headache eased. But one summer day, her life was almost lost in the water of a lake, and that brief scare had ripple effects for my sister and I.

Mother had never learned to swim but going into shallow water she felt safe. On this hot summer day at the lake, she climbed aboard a large inner-tube and was having great fun with my sister standing right beside her. Before long, she decided it was time to get off the inner-tube and out of the water. Thinking she was safe, she shifted her body off the inner-tube to sadly discover that directly under her was a deep hole. Sinking below the surface of the water there, she began to drown. Thankfully through quick action she was saved. I wish this scare had prompted her to take lessons. Instead, mother wanted for us the thing she didn't have, the ability to swim. Though she denied herself this knowledge, she was determined that my sister and I would never feel helpless like she had that day in the water.

Traumatic events are like that. When trauma is experienced we can choose to avoid personal growth by avoiding the thing that has caused it and we can unknowingly infect those around with behaviors or actions that either promote growth or prevent growth. In my mother's case the negative lake experience prevented growth for herself. She allowed that traumatic event to cause her fear and stop her from acting in her own best interest. She never learned to swim.

We are not called by God to live a life dominated by paralyzing fear. Sometimes we just need to feel the fear and move through it with actions that bring us growth. But there are times when danger is present and we shouldn't ignore it by standing, staying, or swimming in it's path...don't swim in shark infested waters!

This scripture speaks this truth.

Proverbs 22:3

The prudent see danger and take refuge, but the simple keep going and pay the penalty.

I am thankful that my mother's life was saved that day on the lake and she was given many more years with us. God knew I needed her. God also knew I needed my Grandpa.

Growing up in their home I'm not sure why my sister and I were told to call Ruel Pendleton, Grandpa. Maybe it was because he was nine years older than his wife and for people in the community where we lived it felt better to the Pendletons that we should designate him in this way.

One thing is for sure about my Grandpa, I came to love him. He was quiet, and held a strength I'm not sure even those within his immediate family understood.

As a younger man and father, tales were told that he had a harsh way with his children, Wilma and Wanda. But in his later years, and by the time I came into the home, the harsh exterior was gone and only a quiet demeanor remained.

In spite of the fact that he had glaucoma and a hearing loss, he was determined to worship the Lord on Sunday.

When I was a teenager, I will never forget the day I asked this question of my mother. "Why does Grandpa even go to Church? He can't see what's going on, he can't hear the songs being sung, why does he even bother?" My mother replied, "Because he wants people to know where he stands." What a testimony to my young heart! This lesson was priceless.

Aside from these trips into town for worship, in the later years of his life, his days were mostly spent there at home in his room, and sitting in his chair by the window. While sitting there he would spend countless hours listening to books recorded for the blind and ballgames on the radio. Only a solitary trip out the back door, down the steps to the garage, and the old refrigerator there interrupted his routine. At least once a day he could be observed coming back from exploring the contents of the refrigerator outside with a bottle of cold Dr. Pepper tucked and hidden in the side pocket of his overalls.

It was only on rare occasions that I was witness to his exercise routine that was limited to him doing chin-ups outside using the carport overhead supports. In this regard, he was still very strong.

I don't have any memory of Grandpa ever eating breakfast but twice daily he would rise from his chair to go to the table to eat lunch and supper. When I look back on his later days, they were solitary..so solitary it makes me sad.

In the summer months, while still in his seventies, Grandpa could be seen attempting to trim back the thorny wild roses along the fence line. Having been blinded in an accident as a younger man and plagued by glaucoma, he remained undeterred in his attempts to mow the yard and trim the roses. These courageous attempts to trim the roses were resisted by the thorns of the roses as they ravaged his skin and tore his shirt in bloody patches. But Grandpa was persistent which was the thing I so admired about him.

One time mother was particularly upset with him for trimming the stately pines that were against the front of the house. His attempt at trimming pine trees while having limited eyesight was a challenge and though he meant well, his attempt went badly and left the pines even crying, never to be the same.

Though the damage to Grandpa's eyesight was limiting for him and at times dangerous for the roses and the pines within the yard, one day, the loss of sight presented a life threatening danger for him.

On this particular day, he decided to venture over a ladder built across a fence that on one side was our yard and upon climbing would get him into the pasture land north of the house. Unfortunately for him, once over the ladder and having traveled a short distance away, he couldn't find his way back home.

Mother, after a time, realizing he wasn't in his room, and not finding him in the garage, began to search. She thankfully found him standing out of the boundary of the fenced yard, in the north pasture.

There he stood frozen, clothed in his overalls and flannel shirt standing in the tall weeds. With poor eyesight and the inability to realize that he was facing the opposite direction of the house, with a weakened voice he was shouting for help. If he had traveled much further, he would've fallen off into a creek.

I'm so thankful that God protected him. I know without a doubt a Godly nudge prompted my mother to go looking for him.

I know he must have felt such relief when she touched his arm to say, " I am here," as she turned him back toward home.

We all need that touch. That touch that reassures us that we're safe, found, and seen. A touch that leads us toward home. In my life, I've experienced God's loving touch through the kindness of others and have been nudged by Him too.

God is good and kind and I thank Him for all the ways he has nudged me in life to check on someone, and take action by stepping into the world of someone who is hurting. God had nudged people toward me too and has sent comfort to my grief stricken heart.

Though Grandpa's pasture adventure was life threatening and dangerous, there were light hearted moments too. One of those occurred on a hot summer day in July.

Days in July in southern Oklahoma were notoriously hot and July fourth brought fireworks that terrified me and sparklers that didn't. Sometimes it even brought something sweet to eat.

On one hot July day, it became my mother's desire to make homemade ice cream. In those days, this process was hard work by strong men who could turn the crank that was attached to a wooden bucket. Within the bucket a metal container sat suspended and was filled with a milky egg concoction that mother had created. Once these steps were complete, chunks of ice and rock salt were sandwiched in the space between the interior sides of the wooden bucket and the exterior sides of the metal container. Then the hard work of turning the crank attached to the bucket would begin with mother adding ice as needed along with rock salt. On this particularly hot day, the job of turning the crank went to my Grandpa, who though aging, still was very strong.

In contrast to those of us on the patio wearing shorts and short sleeve shirts to survive the heat of the day, Grandpa stood in the heat wearing his shirt and heavy overalls. Even in summer, his body temperature trended toward being cold due to his age.

We were bystanders of the process; the loud noisy production of ice cream making. With mouths watering in anticipation, those of us privileged to watch, knew that even though we did nothing to bring it about, we would be rewarded with a heaping bowl of cold goodness soon.`

When the homemade vanilla ice cream was ready to eat, mother would bring bowls and spoons for us all and we would gather there beside the container of ice cream so that she could fill our bowls and our bellies.

I'll never forget the moment while churning the ice cream there on that patio a mouse ran up grandpa's overalls with a cat in hot pursuit. I've never seen anyone exit overalls so fast. I'm not sure who was the most relieved to be free of those overalls, the cat, the mouse or my grandpa. Fortunately......they all lived.

Another interesting thing to know about my grandpa was that he was hard of hearing and with that issue came an occasional instance of confusion over someone's name.

He was sitting at the small round table in the kitchen one day eating his lunch when he looked at me and said, "Sar", in his country accent, "Is Steve with you?" I am not certain where the name Steve came from. I had never dated anyone named Steve. But... my grandpa became convinced my boyfriend's name was Steve. Neither of us ever corrected my grandpa out of compassion, respect, and love.

Each time my boyfriend, a.k.a. Steve came to see me, he would sit at the kitchen table for a chat with my grandpa. I know my grandpa liked talking with Steve, so did I.

The week before my wedding to "Steve", I sat one more time, as a seventeen year old girl, at the bar stool there in the kitchen and asked mother for recipe after recipe which I recorded in a small recipe book I had. These recipes now are old, well worn, food splattered and faded, and the memories associated with each one are treasured by me today.

Mother and grandpa were an inspiration to me. Their long married life and a life of service to others and me in particular remain powerful examples today. I long to see them again. I long to run into their arms with loving thanks for the love, the warm bed, the lap of comfort, their loving examples of what a life for Christ looks like, and the home they provided that no one else would.

Grandpa died October 27th, 1985, at the age of eighty-nine and mother died January 3rd, 2000, at the age of ninety-five. I love and miss them everyday.

CHAPTER 5

MIKE DUNN, MY NEW DAD

Fathers, do not exasperate your
Children; instead, bring them up in
The training and instruction of the
Lord.

—Ephesians 6: 4

What can I say about my new dad except that I loved him. He was so different from the father I had known in every way. He grew up in the Healdton, Oklahoma area, one of thirteen children of Mr. and Mrs. Aaron Dunn. He attended high school in Healdton where he received his diploma. Within a short time of graduating, he married his sweetheart, Wanda Pendleton.

With no education beyond high school, he made his living as a pumper in the oil fields of southern Oklahoma working for the Cox and Hammond Oil Company. Though he spent his days working in the oil fields, he was a country loving cowboy through and through. There was never a time I saw him without his cowboy boots on or his cowboy hat.

He was a Christian, but in all the years I lived at home, he never attended church with us except for one time when we were vacationing in Ruidoso, New Mexico. I don't even know what prompted him to go that day.

It is a mystery to me what exact event or series of events happened to turn him against church attendance. He was definitely determined to let us all know that he was above it all where that was concerned.

To complicate the matter, the known imperfections of people who attended church continued to fuel his negative opinions and he became determined to show us all that he felt fine without going to worship.

It was only later in life, he began going to church services with Wanda on a regular basis. I don't know why except that maybe by this time, his stubborn will had finally weakened. God only truly knows.

He was a hard working cowboy who spent hours behind the wheel of his truck going to oil well sites. I feel certain that the reason it took him hours was the fact that he drove his truck so slow. Whenever I rode with him the pickup's speed never exceeded twenty five miles per hour. This lack of urgency, though it drove me crazy, may be why he lived so long. He never seemed to be in a hurry.

In his spare time, dad cared for all the animals the homestead could contain, which included, two horses, innumerable cows, countless chickens, pigs, rabbits, donkeys, and miniature goats. Beside all the farm animals to care for through the years, there was a cat named Goody, a dog named Earl, a boxer named Dutchie, a dog named Lucky, and a poodle named Zsa Zsa. We could have sold tickets to the zoo in our yard and pasture.

In fact there were so many animals and people at home, my mother, at times in trying to recall my name, in frustration would start down the list of names, Wilma, Wanda, including some-times, Zsa Zsa, the dog, in that list, before hitting correctly upon my name, Sarah. I'm praying I don't repeat this kind of list with my children and grandchildren someday but finding the humor in it, realize there were certainly a lot of names to remember.

As a result of having horses, my sister and I were always itch-ing to ride them but the quarter horse we owned was off limits leaving the small Shetland pony in our sights.

Only on occasion would dad give in to our request to ride Fuzzy because there is some labor involved in getting a horse ready to ride and in fact, it is dangerous to ride a horse that has hardly ever been ridden.

So on those rare days that dad would bring Fuzzy into the yard ready for us to ride, I would climb into the saddle and grab the reins with glee. I loved the experience of riding him, but Fuzzy was no ordinary horse. He was a clever horse soul who would try to scrape riders off by getting close to a fence post gate and if that didn't work, could buck a person off. And yes…I was that person.

While riding him one day with my sister in the front and me sitting behind her, I inadvertently placed my heels in Fuzzy's flanks. What was a fun time became a wild ride as he began to buck and it didn't take long before I was sent flying off. This short ride taught me a great lesson of what not to do when riding toward the back end of a horse. Like the lesson I learned while riding our horse, some lessons in life only come when you climb aboard for the ride.

When I was older, on occasion, dad would take my sister and I with him to the hay fields where sometimes we would take turns sitting behind the wheel of the truck. Dad would let us steer the truck along the cut rows while he loaded the hay onto the back.

Imagine our delight in being allowed to drive and steer the hay truck! I learned to drive a vehicle that had a stick shift long before I took my driver's test.

Country life was an adventure and an education but unfortunately this early driving knowledge and experience though fun, didn't help me to pass the driver's test given at Driver's Ed. Feeling embarrassed and humbled, I watched my friends receive their driver's permits and wished to disappear in a hole in the floor. If only one would open up!

My fifteen year old mind began to slowly understand some things are not accomplished in a straight line. Failure is only failure if you never will yourself to get up and try again and is an excellent teacher if you are willing to learn it's lessons.

With the knowledge I needed to study more, and determination, I set about the task of doing just that. I studied harder.

After finally passing the test and getting my license. I was allowed to drive. Soon after, dad purchased a car for me from a sweet elderly neighbor who could no longer drive. This was no ordinary car, it was magical. I was transported back in time as I climbed into the seat of the most beautiful, baby blue, 1952 Plymouth I'd ever seen.

No one at school had one like it. It had a hood that came down a short way over the front windshield and an acrylic object that was attached to the inside front dash of the car. Sitting left of the wheel, this acrylic object was meant to help the driver see the traffic stoplight change. Unlike the modern cars my friends drove, this car had the largest wheel I'd ever seen and most definitely was not an automatic. It was awesome.

I appreciated the love and care dad gave in the selection of this car for my short use and I drove it with pride feeling happy and free but sometimes I had trouble getting it into reverse, and once I had the terror of driving it home from town with no brakes. This didn't keep me from loving the days I was allowed to drive it. When I got married and moved away the car stayed behind as it wasn't mine to keep. I only wish I had given it a name!

During the years growing up, when summertime came, on occasion, dad would ask us where we wanted to go for vacation but most of the time the vacation destination would already be set. If the grownups wanted to stay closer to home we would travel to camp at a state park not far from our home and only fifty miles away located in Sulphur, Oklahoma. These camping trips were an adventure, and as a young child I'd never camped in my life nor floated on an inner tube or played in a stream of water.

Upon finding our campsite, we'd pitch tents and set up cots to sleep on each night. Each morning mother would cook a delicious breakfast of bacon and eggs over a hot campfire. This was her domain, her area of expertise, and we knew she required no help from us as she proceeded to cook our breakfast.

The smell of the bacon cooking in the cast iron pan would drift through the air causing our mouths to water in anticipation.

I loved watching my mother cook, whether at home or when we would camp. I was fascinated watching her remove the bacon that had become perfectly crisp and then break open fresh eggs into the hot bacon grease. This release of the eggs from their shell into the hot grease would cause them to sizzle, pop and dance until they were transformed in the hot pan. As I watched, mother would then spoon the excess bacon grease over their unbroken tops as she saw no need for turning them. Once done, we would fill our plates and gobble down every bite.

Camping sites at Chickasaw National Park were full of people with families just like us trying to enjoy time away from their busy work lives within the surrounding towns.

Though the summer days were hot we stayed cooled in the streams of water within the Park as we all jumped in, played and splashed. There we would stay for several hours enjoying the water by floating on large black inner tubes until our hands looked like prunes from staying in the water too long.

After swimming we'd return to our campsite and place our wet towels over the ropes tied between trees knowing the heat of the summer would quickly dry them for the next day's use.

By night, we'd sit in our chairs and look up at the stars, while the campfire lit our faces in a warm glow. The sound of voices of people camping around us and crickets would combine in a melodious hum that continued until the voices ceased and the crickets sang us to sleep. It was so peaceful.

It was believed that the water there in the state park, for which the town was named, contained sulphur and had healing properties. People from everywhere would come and drink from the fountains in the park hoping to receive benefits to their health. The down side was that the water tasted like rotten eggs. I can't imagine what the benefits were, but I drank the water too.

Vacationing together as a family didn't happen every year but it made the times we did travel together memorable and appreciated. I am thankful for our dad's willingness to take us on trips when he could.

Dad was always taking us interesting places as we traveled far away to Carlsbad Caverns in New Mexico, Ruidoso, New Mexico to watch the horse races, and Arkansas.

Closer to home, he took our family to the rodeo in Ardmore, Oklahoma where we watched bull riding, barrel racing, and where sometimes, a real life television star would make a special appearance.

During the Christmas season, dad would take us into town to see the Christmas decorations and Santa. The Main Street, lined on each side by shops was always decorated with festive garland and red bows while shop owners decorated their shop windows beckoning shoppers to come inside and get out of the cold.

Parents hoping to keep the magic of Christmas alive would line up with their children to sit on Santa's lap. While some children were excited to tell their Christmas wishes, some were scared of the man wearing the large red suit and refused to sit. But not me… I sat every time because there was a candy cane waiting at the end of talking to Santa and I knew it.

Every Christmas Eve, dad, Wanda, and my sister and I, would load up the car with presents to take to Ma and Pa Dunn's house. On this night, my sister and I were always dressed alike in beautiful homemade Christmas dresses made by our mother, and which no store bought dress could rival.

Upon arrival at the Dunn family home, Ma and Pa would be sitting in their symbolic thrones like royalty while their large extended family lovingly gathered and filed past to present them with gifts and kisses.

As parents to so many children, their small home during the Christmas holiday would be overrun by their visiting children, their daughter-in-laws and son-in-laws, and their grandchildren in a noisy, festive joy. I loved them and that family.

After evening festivities at Ma and Pa's we would head back home to Wirt to open our presents waiting there under the Christmas tree. Arriving at home and exiting the car, we'd run inside to find not just one gift under the tree for my sister and me, but many.

Sometimes Wilma, dressed in a Santa suit would go outside and knock on a window in the living room with a hearty HO, HO, HO. This often brought laughter and delight from my sister and I in the actual belief that Santa was at our window.

I'd never had a Christmas gift before this time. When I think back, I know that it was all done in love. I know that my new family sat there in loving anticipation as my sister and I, with wild abandon, tore through every wrapped gift. Our cries of excitement and delight filled the air as each gift was uncovered. Their faces beamed with joy as they watched us.

There was only one Christmas in my memory that didn't turn out as our parents hoped. This particular year we were given a popular item for tree decoration, Angel Hair. Angel Hair is made from spun fiberglass. My sister and I decorated the tree with it and unfortunately we both had bad skin reactions from using it. We were miserable and as a result our parents wisely decided that Angel Hair was forever banned for Christmas tree use.

The only other "out of the ordinary" Christmas occurred many years later after I was married. On this particular Christmas, dad decided to dispense with the traditional purchase of a live Christmas tree. Instead, with creative humor, my dad brought a dead oak tree from the pasture into the house and stuck it in a bucket. When we arrived from Dallas to visit them, there it stood in the living room, in all of it's glory, with ornaments hanging from the bare branches. My dad was so proud.

Throughout my childhood years I felt I had a good relationship with my dad. His actions were loving and sweet as he built things for my sister and I to swing on, play on, and play in. He seemed happy and proud to be our dad.

During my teen years, he continued to do things that he thought would bring us joy. He bought a bicycle built for two for my sister and I, brought store bought clothes for us to try on and keep, and lavished us with Christmas gifts. To an onlooker, it was wonderful.

But amid the gift of things, the atmosphere within our family began to change. He began to be harsh with angry outburst that wounded me with cruel, hate filled words. I was at a loss to understand the change in him and I began to wonder what I had done to bring on his anger. His words always left me feeling unloved and unwanted. In order to cope I began to bury my feelings.

All the while, I was trying to navigate the social minefield of high school, carry on with school work to make good grades, and date the occasional boy of interest that crossed my path.

No matter what I did or said, my dad's behavior continued unchanged as his pattern of behavior continued to include moments of warmth mixed with abusive language and actions. My relationship with him became increasingly difficult and filled with frustration. I never could figure out what the problem was or how to navigate those treacherous waters. There seemed to be nothing I could do to help my dad understand I loved him.

In the end….he broke my heart.

CHAPTER 6

WANDA

Though I speak with the tongues
Of men and of angels, and have not
Charity, I am become as sounding brass,
Or a clanging cymbal.

—I Corinthians 13: 1

The youngest daughter of the Pendletons, was Wanda Dunn. Growing up I was told to say that she was my mother to people at school and church, but within the home and through the years, she went by and answered to many names, some of which were Babe, Baby Jo, Wanda, and Nanny.

Wanda had long dark black hair, which was worn on top of her head in large curls, a popular hairstyle of the time. She had thick black eyelashes and beautiful brown eyes and often wore bright red lipstick that accentuated her beauty.

Like her sister Wilma, she was an artist but she didn't use acrylic oil or paint to create her pictures on canvas as her sister had. Her artwork was just as wonderful as she created beautiful large pictures made from coins, one of which was a large picture of a horse's head. It was incredible. She also used different types of beans and seeds to create a picture of a rooster. It was painstakingly done and absolutely beautiful.

At times, she was an amateur archaeologist and explorer as she ventured outside exploring the land and the creek of the family owned property. Over time through days of exploration of the creek beds on the property, she found ancient arrowheads and collected various old bottles that were of interest and value to her.

She loved plants and loved to display the large red peppers she often brought back from trips to New Mexico as well as the turquoise jewelry she collected through the years. She loved turquoise jewelry and worn against her browned sunbaked skin, she was stunning.

She rarely helped with cooking the main meals within the home but she loved to make sun tea which we all enjoyed. She would fill a gallon jar with water and then place a large tea bag inside. Covering it with a lid, she would then take the jar outside and place it on the top of the cellar during the hot summer days. The sun then did a magical job of heating the water free of charge and brewing the tea perfectly. It always tasted wonderful.

The other thing I watched her do in the kitchen involved the making of sweet things to eat. Each Thanksgiving holiday and Christmas she loved to make coconut date cookies that disappeared quickly when I was around. They were only made during the holidays and were my favorite.

Sometimes in the summer months, she would also make Key Lime Pie. I remember sitting on the stool at the kitchen counter watching her whip the green jello mixture with a hand mixer into a mound of heavenly tasting goodness that was then poured into a pre-baked pie shell. This refrigerator pie was delicious and didn't take long for us as a family to eat every bite. I am so glad I have both recipes today.

Above all, she was absolutely devoted to our mother. These two women spent every afternoon together sitting in the living room of our home crocheting. Between the two of them, mother's closet became filled and stacked with items they had made to be given away.

Unlike mother, who had a warm loving nature, in personality and behavior Wanda was like Forest Gump's box of chocolates, you never knew what you were going to get.

Each day living in her presence was like being on a roller coaster. When I was young and first came into the home, I never saw her behavior be anything that would have given me cause for fear. During the early years, it was a smooth and easy ride. But like a roller coaster that starts slow and tends to build speed with huge dips and swings, her behavior too began to change and she demonstrated episodes of angry frustration at the behaviors of my sister and the things that I did that frustrated her. Knowing how to stay onboard that roller coaster without injury was something I never learned to figure out. Sometimes people are born without the ability to feel emotion or empathy for others but this was not the case for her.

When I look back upon the many behaviors that were peculiar to Wanda I realize that she must have had things happen to her that caused her to be the way she was; events that were never dealt with, buried over time, and held unhealed for decades. She exhibited hidden behaviors at home that were unknown to those friends in the community, the people she saw at worship every Sunday, and all outside of the family. Below all that artistry and beauty, with smiles of greeting and the appearance of good will, was a person dominated by fear and an angry person that could be so cruel.

I'm not qualified to understand what her issues were, nor able to explain, the seething anger that always sat slightly below the surface. I don't know what happened to shape her into someone who seemed to hate others so much. I was witness to her mask of sweetness and light to people greeting her, but the second they left her presence, terrible foul thoughts about them would pour out from her mouth. When people from her church family tried to show her kindness during hospital stays she would act terrible and refuse their visits.

Within the home, her hate-filled thoughts were not held in check and would seep out like poison directed mostly toward my sister and on occasion toward me.

I'll never know what caused the anger she carried, and I'll never understand why the other adult members of our family didn't intervene when she dished out abuse. In that regard they acted in solidarity. No one stepped forward to stop it.

As children, my sister and I were subjected to her cruelty. I saw the whelps she left from the wire end of a fly swatter on my sister's legs as punishment for some infraction she had committed and I felt my big toe enter my sleeping mouth as she forced it there in an aggressive attempt to wake me up.

I was given the chore of washing dishes in the home after our meals. I didn't mind washing the dishes but there were times she would fill the wash tub with soapy, boiling, scalding, hot water. Have you ever tried to pick up a scalding hot wet dishcloth? Scalding water, upon young hands is a bad combination and if I cried out in pain, I'd be shoved aside in disgust or expected to endure.

My first youthful attempts at learning to use the heavy antique iron, which had to be heated on the gas burner on the stove top, often produced frustration and anger for her as she watched my efforts. I wasn't quick in the process of ironing so that the iron would need to be returned to the gas stove top often. These kitchen moments spent with her and being in her presence was like a tightrope walk, you didn't want to fall off.

Even after I married, she displayed unexpected moments of spitting anger over something I had done that made her mad.

One particular episode occurred over a weekend in which Kenneth and I had come home for a short visit and stay. With our intention of going on vacation the following week, our first night there started off great. But during the night, Kenneth began to feel sick and it was downhill from there. He came down with the flu.

Within hours, unfortunately my mother began to be ill as well. I felt terrible knowing she probably had gotten sick as a result of our visit but there was nothing I could have done to prevent it as there was no hint of illness that gave us warning we shouldn't go home. Once there we were unfortunately trapped, unable to leave until Kenneth was well enough to travel.

As mother's illness grew worse and raged on, a gathered, hushed, vigil began by the remaining adults in the kitchen which sat just outside her room. It was while standing there, Wanda turned to me, and in an angry fevered rant screamed, "If mother dies, it will be all your fault."

I stood there stunned into silence at her words. Though I had lived through verbal abuse from her before, this threat carried a deeper injury. My brain screamed within me but my mouth was shut by her accusation in a fearful silence. What could I say? Didn't she know I would never do anything intentionally to cause my mother harm? Then the fear truly set in. How could I ever get over it if I unintentionally caused the death of my mother?

The next few days there at Wirt were filled with an unbearable tension waiting to see if mother would get better and she did. I felt such relief when she began to improve and totally recovered.

Unfortunately, that night stayed with me and I didn't recover from the hateful words or the hateful solidarity of the adults in that moment. No apologies were ever expressed by her or anyone else that night or after for the things that were said. What I was left with was the cold understanding that my feelings were of no consequence; they didn't matter and would never matter.

Wanda displayed her fears in other ways too. She was deathly afraid of spiders and stormy weather.

I remember the exact day her fear of spiders came about. While she was cleaning a storage building on our property a fiddleback spider crawled up her leg. She was not aware of the danger until she felt it's bite. Within hours of the poisonous bite, she saw the symptom of red streaks climbing up her leg. Fortunately she knew to seek treatment quickly, and it saved her life. Though she would live, her recovery was long and what was left was a huge wound that rotted the flesh on her thigh and the absolute fear of being bitten again.

Wanda was also afraid of the storms that came yearly and seasonally as spring storms in southern Oklahoma happen often bringing high winds, rain, and on occasion the chance of tornadoes. With any storm, day or night, she took no chances. Her fear would reign affecting us all. At her urging, en masse, we would exit the house to take refuge in the shelter of our damp underground cellar.

As young, innocent children, my sister and I secretly liked these escapes to the stormy cellar only because it gave us childhood delight in being given the opportunity to light the lantern. We often raced to see who could get there first. The winner of that race would carefully remove the lantern's glass cover, and strike the match to set the lantern's wick aflame. Then the glass cover would carefully be replaced and light would be sent into the dark corners within the cellar illuminating our faces in a soft glow.

The cellar was enclosed by a wood and metal door weighted by a cement block that was attached to the door by a chain. Huddled there in the damp cellar, with the light from the kerosene lantern, we'd all sit in the tension of the storm, listening for the thunder and corresponding lightning strike and counting the space in-between in attempts to determine how far away the strike was. Minutes seemed like hours while we sat on the wood benches or chairs waiting for the storm to pass. When the storm was over Wanda, the other adults, my sister and I, and even once a dog, would exit the storm shelter to see that the sun would be shining through the gray clouds and, as in life, an occasional rainbow.

Unfortunately, unhealthy family dynamics played out sometimes when storms required a trip to the cellar. Sometimes the decision was made to leave grandpa behind in the house. Mother would decide it was too difficult for him to make the stairs down into the cellar though he, without assistance, daily went down the back porch steps. There was no argument from a soul about why we shouldn't flee to the cellar, or worse yet, why we shouldn't leave grandpa behind.

Instead, when storms came, depending on the whims of convenience, he would be left behind in the house while we selfishly went on without him down into the cellar to escape the storms that raged around us. This fact now breaks my heart.

How do you ever get to such a point that you as a family, devalue the life of a member within the family? This was a pattern of behavior from this family directed toward him long before I came into the home and one that continued during my childhood and after.

It was common for him to be left at home while we would vacation. He always sat isolated in his room and apart from his family most of the day while at home, and received no warmth or affection that I can ever remember from his wife or grown daughters.

I wish now I had spoken up on his behalf, told him often he was loved by me, hugged his neck and while holding his hand, helped him down into the cellar. Unfortunately, I just didn't know then what I know and understand now.

Wanda's frequent display of fear during stormy weather became contagious and spread into my young heart like a virus. The tales of a female relative whose life had been lost in a tornado while she was at school added to my fear and gave me nightmares and anxiety that affected me for a long time. Though I no longer have this fear, I recognize when other dangers are present and I wisely seek shelter.

Another curiosity about Wanda was that there were many years that she chose to never be home for her birthday which came at the end of the month of May. No opportunity was given for those of us within the home to celebrate with her this special day. She and dad would always travel to Ruidoso, New Mexico, where they would spend her birthday, celebrating it away from us all. It was where she was happiest, I think.

Wanda and dad loved spending time in Ruidoso, New Mexico. They loved escaping the summertime heat of Oklahoma to rest and recuperate from the constant care of livestock, oil field work and monotony of life at home.

After traveling there for several years, they decided to purchase a small cabin which they renovated in the hopes that it would enable them to stay there for longer periods of time and they loved it.

Ruidoso for them, became a perfect escape with mountain cabin living and the horse races that they loved to watch there.

In the summertime, rain would come off the mountain in the afternoon, just long enough to wet the ground and then would stop. The nights there were cool verging on cold which felt good coming from the blazing one hundred degree heat of Southern Oklahoma.

In time, they began driving to Ruidoso in September to be there during the Labor Day horse races as well and as the years passed, close friends from Oklahoma came to join them. Their small cabin made it possible for them to stay longer and they began to do just that.

Being fearlessly independent and while in their nineties, dad drove himself and Wanda to Ruidoso taking all the back roads they could find. He wasn't able to see well and neither did Wanda. I can still picture it in my mind. These two sight impaired elderly folks, determined to still travel to their vacation paradise, fearlessly driving down the street like Mr. Magoo, while people in other cars dodged the car with the Ragtown license plate. I'm thankful they never got hurt or hurt someone else on these trips. Definitely in these moments, God was there protecting them and everyone else.

As Wanda grew older she began to change, and at times seemed softer in her later years. I was filled with compassion for her and the situation she found herself in and hated that at times when we visited she would cry and was sad.

One of the most heart breaking days for me with her occurred after my sister placed her in a nursing home and I had come to visit her. As I entered her room I could see that she had packed all of her things and had placed them against the wall. She looked at me with relief and said, " Sarah, I am so glad you came to take me home. I knew you would come." My heart sank, as I heard her words knowing there would be no rescue that day. I had no legal power to intervene, though for years, I had wanted with all of my heart to take her, dad and Wilma home with me. When I first asked them to join us in Stillwater, Oklahoma they weren't ready to leave their homes and then when it came time that they could no longer live at home and it would've been better for them to be with us, I didn't have the power of attorney to do so.

When I think about her now my heart is filled with forgiveness. I choose to pour it all over her actions of abuse, physical and verbal that were directed towards me. Because, in spite of it all, I loved her. I wish now I could have spent the last moments of her life with her, holding her hand and telling her that I loved her. She was God's child and loved by him and so loved by me.

She died June, 21st, 2019, at the age of ninety-five. She was buried in a cemetery in Healdton, Oklahoma. One year and five months later, on November 18, 2020, at the age of ninety-eight, dad would join her there.

I loved them both.

CHAPTER 7

WONDERFUL WILMA

Give her honor for all that her hands
Have done. Let everything she has done
Bring praise to her at the city gate.

—Proverbs 31:31

What do I say about the person that held such a special place in my heart except there isn't a day that goes by that I don't wish she was still here.

From the beginning of my entry into the home of the Pendleton family, Wilma and I shared a room.

Her days started early in the morning with regular exercise as I often woke to find her doing leg lifts on the floor at the end of our twin beds. She then would dress for work and leave the house for her job in town. At the end of the work day in town she would return home, change clothes, and continue to help mother by mopping the tiled floors or working outside in the flowerbeds.

Though she was the oldest daughter of Gladys and Ruel Pendleton, she certainly didn't have the characteristics of a typical first born child. Quiet and introverted, she almost went unnoticed in any social situation. She had worn glasses from an early age and, unlike the dark striking features of her younger sister, had brown hair with features that favored her father Ruel.

It's fascinating to me how events in childhood can shape the life and heart of a person. But what is more fascinating to me is how Wilma and Wanda, raised in the same home and environment, could be so strikingly different in behavior and character.

Though to the casual observer Wilma may not have been viewed as a beauty, she was beautiful in all the ways that truly mattered. She was cheerful with a heart that was loving, unselfish and mostly kind. Like the rest of the world, she wasn't perfect and there were moments in which she, like her sister Wanda, veered off course.

Through all of the early years we had spent together I loved her, trusted her, and believed she loved me. I still do. But one particular day, one rare episode of verbal abuse by her, directed toward me, wounded my heart and affected me so deeply that her words became branded in my heart.

As often with the verbal abuse that occurred within the home, it seemed like an average day. It hadn't been filled with any drama that I was aware of or any drama that I had created. On this particular day, Wilma walked up to me and said in an angry outburst that they were all sorry that they had ever brought my sister and me into their home and that we had been nothing but a heartache to them. I was a teenager at this point and I responded to her cruel words as I always had when assaulted with verbal abuse that happened within the home...I stood in stunned silence.

What do you do when you are without power in a situation not of your choosing? I was devastated that she felt compelled to deliver this message in this way and her verbal assault felt like such a betrayal of the close relationship I believed we shared. Did I blame her? No. Did I blame myself? Yes.

How did I respond after I received this knowledge? I felt guilty that I could not be what or who they would want as a child and I tried harder to change myself in an effort to be loved.

Though this frequent pattern of abusive behavior continued throughout the years by other members of the family, Wilma rarely was a participant.

Because our relationship had been strong and had been built over years of time with only rare episodes of abuse from her, these insults were easily forgiven and I loved her. Whenever we were home to visit, I was eager to spend time with her and looked for her the moment we entered the house.

Of all the things Wilma was, she was also a mother to me. Though she never married or gave birth to children, she was as much a mother to me as anyone else in the home where I grew up. The early years we spent together and later became instrumental in cementing a bond between us that lasted until the day she died.

Wilma loved being outside, going on what she called "nature walks", or just sitting on the front porch looking up at the night sky. Wilma, the worker bee, was never too busy to spend time with me.

Magical warm summer nights were spent together, just Wilma and me, on the front porch. Nights that were often a mixture of war and symphony as we battled the mosquitoes while bathed in the night sounds of crickets chirping.

Unobscured by city lights, we could see every star in the heavens and would watch the night sky for shooting stars. Nature also provided tiny blinking lights as the mating dance of lightning bugs would illuminate the yard and trees in a glorious splendor. My sister and I would run in delight with glass jars in hand trying to capture as many as we could to have a closer view of their display.

These wonderful, unforgettable summer night moments with Wilma are the ones I'll never forget.

Her life was filled with work and activity at home that prioritized being healthy and she wanted that for the ones she loved. She would often have mother and me join her in walking the country miles for exercise.

During my teen years we spent every afternoon after I would get home from school walking the one mile stretch of section line that sat west of our home. By the time we returned home we would have two miles worth of exercise done for the day. Often the three of us would start that walk side by side but after a time I would walk, and then run that stretch of road trying to beat them home.

The best part was that no gym dues were needed, no monthly payments to an exercise coach were spent. It was just healthy, sweat producing, country living that didn't cost anything but our effort.

Wilma wisely knew that putting the effort in was the cost and always brought rewards within your spirit, if nowhere else.

She was an artist and painted beautiful works of art on canvas that were proudly displayed in our home but as she aged, her eyesight failed her and the thing she once loved to do was lost to her.

When we were young, she loved to take photographs of our family outings and events and due to her efforts many important moments long gone were captured and today bring me memories of happy times spent with them.

All the creative things within me I attribute to Wilma. My love for photography, my love for interior design, my love for drawing horses and trees as a child, and my love for learning came from those moments spent with her.

Her example of always learning something new and interest in doing new things prompted her to learn how to write using calligraphy which resulted in the beautiful letters she sent out. She often sent letters of thanks and letters that expressed love and kindness for others. On rare occasions, she sent out letters directed at me that expressed anger over something that had upset her and when they arrived at my home, I hated receiving them. Fortunately I received very few of those.

Wilma, after high school worked to get her beautician's license and used her acquired knowledge and skills to wash, cut, and style the hair of the women in our home.

Her love for me was showcased on the day of my wedding as she washed and painstakingly pin curled my hair. When it was dried and released from the pins, it looked beautiful and hung in glorious curls, beneath my veil.

On another occasion after I was married, I came home for a visit and I asked Wilma if she could cut my hair but this day at the home salon would almost be a disaster. As she proceeded to cut my hair, my short hair became shorter and shorter. I sat quietly spellbound as the cutting continued unable to say a word. Before long she put the scissors down … job complete. When she was done, let me say, it was short….really short.

Within moments of setting her scissors down, she exclaimed loudly, " OH MY COW….I had the wrong glasses on!"

When the haircut is free what can you do but say thank you and smile with a note to self….next time make sure Wilma checks which glasses need to be worn for the job! I never complained, knowing hair grows back, and I laugh when I think about that day.

After my children were born, Wilma the worker bee always had time for them. When we would come to my childhood home to visit, she would gather my children up and take them on nature walks on the property.

Her loving nature always shined bright during those years but over time, Wilma forgot that she had needs too. In an effort to make sure our mother's needs were met and her remaining years were pleasant, Wilma devoted herself so entirely in that pursuit that she neglected going to the doctor herself. As a result, she became unaware that she was losing her eyesight and eventually it became too late for anything more to be done to save it.

After the death of our mother, with hearing fading and eyesight lost to glaucoma, she became very much like her father Ruel, quiet and secluded, removed from the members of her family.

In her later years, she mostly lived alone in the big house we had all shared but during the day, Wanda and dad would walk from their home down the hill to sit in the living room watching the television that Wilma could no longer see nor hear.

At lunch time, they would gather in the small kitchen to share their lunch hour and then dad and Wanda would retire back to the living room for more television watching or naps in their chairs.

Late afternoon, Wanda and dad would return back to their home on the hill and the house would return to a lonely quiet.

On occasion, if we came for a visit, Wilma could often be found sitting alone in a room apart from her sister and brother-in-law or found outside spending time in a makeshift office that had been created for her on the property.

Even in her later years, her work ethic never faded as she would still attempt to do housework even though her eyesight was virtually gone. I even once returned home for a visit to find her on her hands and knees trying to clean the floor by hand.

She never complained or bemoaned her situation and bravely struggled on. She was amazing.

When my daughters married, she was there at their weddings. When my grandchildren were born, she delighted in their arrivals.

Later in life, Wilma lived with Kenneth and me in our home in Stillwater, Oklahoma. Wilma only lived a few short weeks with us and then was summoned home. We so enjoyed her being with us.

Change is hard on a family and in spite of the love and care given to her within our home, my dad called to say that they wanted her to come back to Wirt.

She told us that she didn't want to go and was happy. But, Wilma was never one to put her needs above the needs of others and to keep the peace within the family, she had us take her home.

I was heartbroken that she felt she had to return to a home that was overrun with mice and had ceilings damaged with huge cracks that posed a serious danger of caving in. There were other dangers too. She had already had one intruder into the home while she was alone there but this event was dismissed and disregarded by my dad.

While living with us, we had also discovered that Wilma had breast cancer and needed treatment which she quickly received due to our daughter Cara's help. But when called to return home, that care and treatment in Stillwater stopped as she again put her needs last.

In spite of these dangers, we were powerless to intervene and sadly, were forced to take her back home.

It wasn't long after her return home, she fell and was placed in a local nursing home. The remaining years of her life were spent there and during the time of Covid much time was spent alone in her room in isolation. She couldn't receive visitors. When I finally was able to go in and see her she exclaimed, "My dream has come true. You are here. I thought you were mad at me." It was heartbreaking.

Eventually the restriction on my visits to her were lifted and I had the privilege of holding her hand, in the last hours of her life. I whispered in her ear how much I loved her and cried my eyes out when the nursing home called to say she had passed away a few hours later.

I'm so thankful for the Godly nudge that God gave me the previous night to travel down from Tulsa to Wilson, Oklahoma, to the nursing home where she lived. She was everything to me.

When I think about Wilma, tears often come along with the thought....I still hope I live a life that would make her proud.

She died May 28, 2021, at the age of ninety-nine.

CHAPTER 8

NOTHING WASTED

After all, what is Apollos? And what is
Paul? We are only people who serve.
We helped you to believe. The Lord
Has given each of us our own work
To do. I planted the seed. Apollos
Watered it. But God has been making
It grow.

—I Corinthians 3: 5-6

The southern part of the United States is known as the Bible Belt and where we lived there was a strong Christian community and the family that raised me, believed wholeheartedly in going to church, with one exception, my new dad.

Winter, spring, summer, and fall, every Sunday morning, Sunday night and Wednesday night was spent by the rest of our family in bible class, or worship within the Shell St. Church of Christ building in Healdton, Oklahoma.

During Sunday morning worship, when I was little, I'd sit snuggled beside my mother. When I got a little older I would sit with my best friend, Jeannie Jones. While the adults, worshiped and sang, Jeannie and I often sat together comparing the freckles on our knees, giggling, and talking. It was the last item that often got me into trouble.

One unfortunate Sunday, my mother noticed I was talking too much to my friend Jeannie in church and I had to make the horrifying walk of shame back to the family pew. Another lesson learned.

But in life, some lessons are better caught than taught and come about as the result of a life lived before you that demonstrates goodness to such a degree that you want to imitate the behavior.

Every year sweet couples from church would bring birthday gifts just for me but this was not the only gift they delivered. Whether they realized it or not, their love poured over me during those years became deeply planted in my heart. Their seeds of kindness have grown in my heart producing perennial actions that have continuously bloomed, grown, and produced fruit today.

I wish I had one more day with these sweet souls to tell them of my love for them. I wish I could say thank you just once more for the love they poured over my broken heart.

Through the years, attendance at church provided another kind of family. This family was built upon the united belief in God and a life dedicated to Christ. This spiritual environment provided the ability to meet and know other children, their families, and those senior couples whose children were grown and gone from home. The worship building was always full, front to back, with people from all walks of life that lived in our small town.

During the summer months when children were out of school, other opportunities for gaining bible knowledge were provided for younger children in the local church building through VBS (vacation bible school), but the older children were encouraged to go to a church camp that was not far from our home.

Children under the age of thirteen were not considered old enough to go to this particular camp and so when I finally reached the required age, I was beyond excited at the opportunity to go to camp. Knowing that my sister would be there with me certainly helped me not feel totally alone and gave a certain level of comfort to my inexperienced heart.

Being a first time camper can be overwhelming and I had questions. Questions like, Will I make friends? Will I be able to sleep at night and not be afraid? What if I find a boy I like there and he doesn't like me? .....even worse....What if I don't like the food? OH..THE..HORRORS!

With youthful energy we loaded the car with the necessary towels, clothing, suitcases and bedding, along with box fans, bug spray, and sunscreen meant to help us survive the July heat, sun, and mosquitoes.

Filled with the mystery of what life at camp might hold for my sister and me, excitement built as we finally got into the car with our parents to make the journey to camp. Our parents were excited too, but for entirely different reasons.

In what seemed like a heartbeat, we pulled into the camp parking lot along with other families bringing their children.

Sooner Youth Camp, established in 1947, was located only forty short miles from our home at Lake Murray State Park, outside of Ardmore, Oklahoma. Situated only a short walking distance from the lake's shore, this camp had two large divided areas with cabins. One area for the boy's cabins and one area of girl's cabins that was strictly monitored by watchful adults. Activity areas of the camp included a softball field, ping pong tables that were often in demand and a place where adults and children could play horse shoes. All activities inspired spirited competition and included frequent breaks to the canteen that served cold drinks and treats for the campers. Best of all, the camp had a large dining hall that was staffed by women who volunteered to cook and feed the hungry campers each week.

There at Sooner daily bible lessons were taught during the mornings, while every night children gathered to worship and sing. This rich environment echoed with sounds of worship along with a noisy chorus of cicadas that sang from the trees. Preachers brought lessons of faith while we, campers and counselors, gathered there each night to worship and discover faith for ourselves.

There were many nights at camp where I saw boys and girls who decided to dedicate their lives to God after listening to the dynamic sermons that spoke of Jesus and His love for us by giving His life on a cross.

On these nights, all of the campers and counselors would walk down to the lake to witness the demonstrations of obedient faith in Christ by the fellow campers who walked into the water there to be baptized. The warm night air was filled with glorious worship songs that echoed across the lake while car lights and evening stars illuminated the believers who entered into the darkened water. This brief but complete immersion in water, this burial, was and is symbolic of the death of Christ, in that the person baptized dies to their past way of living, and is symbolic of the resurrection of Christ, as those baptized rise from the water to live a new life.

But, I didn't join those who went forward asking to be baptized at camp. My baptism had occurred two years before with a water experience that varied greatly from those at Sooner Youth Camp and the difference couldn't have been more profound.

Unlike the youth at camp, my baptism was devoid of any deep emotion. I had no knowledge or realization that I was lost and certainly didn't feel sinful and in need of a Savior.

My baptism was the result of the pressure exerted by my well meaning but overeager parents during the week of a Gospel meeting held at our church building.

Gospel meetings were common and popular in the Bible Belt in the 1960's. In our church home in southern Oklahoma these arranged events consisted of nightly meetings that lasted a week and included visiting preachers that were invited from outside of the local body of believers to present the nightly lessons. Growing up, we never missed a Gospel meeting in town and sometimes those held at other churches and congregations that were out of town.

In the fall of 1966, our church held another Gospel meeting and the preacher chosen to come bring the lessons each night was loved and highly respected by my family.

With this knowledge, our parents approached my sister and I with more than a request. They wanted us both to go forward and be baptized on the last night of this meeting.

I was eleven years old and thought, why not. I always wanted to please my parents. I also liked the idea of being able to drink the juice and eat the crackers that were passed down the rows every Sunday morning like the grown ups and some of the older children I knew. Sadly, the deeper meaning behind all of these actions had escaped me.

I'd sat on these church pews since the age of four, had attended all the Bible classes, knew Jesus was God's son, sang the songs everyone sang and knew that getting baptized would please my parents, so up the aisle, to the front of the church building on Friday night I went. Up to the front where I confessed my belief that Jesus was God's son. Up to the baptistry where I was to be lowered under the water.

The water was warm, my heart was expecting juice and crackers, and I was too young.

True love for Christ and a full understanding of the sacrifice Christ paid for me was still years away. Well meaning though they were, what my parents didn't realize or comprehend was that faith in Christ couldn't be orchestrated for me by them.

Faith in Christ needed to be up to me and the decision to be baptized due to a full understanding of what that decision means. Being lowered under the water doesn't necessarily make one a Christian, as sitting in a cockpit doesn't make you a pilot. I just got wet.

During the next seven years, I continued to read and study the Bible. I attended church on Sunday morning and Sunday night. I attended Wednesday night bible classes. I continued to go to Sooner Youth Camp in the summertime and attended the gospel meetings held at our church building.

The love shown me by my church family wasn't wasted. The years spent and lessons learned from the pulpit and within the classrooms at Shell Street Church of Christ weren't wasted either. These were faith building years that were spent singing songs to God in worship while sitting beside my parents and my best friend Jeannie. Years where the building was full of people who loved the Lord and poured love into my life through their actions and deeds.

Almost seven years would pass after my baptismal event and it was in that same building, the building, where years of time had been spent in the classrooms there that I would make a different kind of commitment.

September 8th, 1973, I married the love of my life there within it's walls. My married life began and I left forever my childhood home and the church home where the foundations of my faith were laid.

It was only a few short weeks later I made the decision to be baptized again. I completely understood my need for a Savior, and in knowing that, it brought about an urgency that I had never experienced before. With a thankful heart I stepped once more into the water of a baptistry and devoted my life to God. Once again the water was warm, my heart was thankful, and this time I was mature.

God's servants had been planting the seed and watering it all of my young life but God had made it grow in my heart. I am thankful for everyone who planted and watered. Their efforts were not wasted by me and I thank God for them.

CHAPTER 9

SATAN'S MASQUERADE PARTY

….For Satan masquerades as
An angel of light.

—2 Corinthians 11: 14

t often can be hard to understand the way that God is working in the life of a person but you can be certain He is working.

As there is no way to pull back the curtain and know what God is doing behind the scenes of a life, we may find ourselves afraid and begin to try to take the reins and be our own god to make things work out the way we think is best.

The recorded story of creation found in the book of Genesis, along with the creation account of Adam and Eve, gives great insight into what happens when we play god in our lives and serves to remind mankind exactly who God is and who we are not. In addition it allows us to gain wisdom and insight into the role that fear can play in our lives and how Satan can use that to undermine our trust in God.

As we take a careful look we see God's loving provision for Adam. He created a beautiful garden where He placed Adam to live. He created beautiful trees within the garden that produced food for Adam to eat. In the center of this new garden home, God placed two special trees; one that produced fruit that was safe to eat, and one that produced fruit that God warned would bring about certain death for the partaker.

Adam is given this warning first.

Genesis 2:15-17

The Lord God took the man and put him in the Garden of Eden to work it and take care of it. And the Lord God commanded the man, "You are free to eat from any tree in the garden; but you must not eat from the tree of the knowledge of good and evil, for when you eat from it you will certainly die."

After God gives this warning to Adam, He sees that it isn't good for Adam to be alone and Eve is lovingly created.

In the very next chapter of Genesis, we see that Eve is fully aware of God's commands and knows there is a tree she must avoid.

Genesis 3: 2

The woman said to the serpent, "We may eat fruit from the trees in the garden, but God did say, "You must not eat fruit from the tree that is in the middle of the garden, and you must not touch it, or you will die."

God, their Creator and Father didn't want them to die. He wanted relationship with them and had given them free will and choice. Most importantly with love, He warned them to avoid eating from the tree that would bring about their deaths. Eve, unfortunately was approached soon after by Satan masquerading as a snake. He played upon her youth and innocence and cleverly paired a truth with a lie.

Genesis 3:4-5

"You will not certainly die," the serpent said to the woman. "For God knows that when you eat from it your eyes will be opened, and you will be like God, knowing good and evil."

As Satan waited in evil anticipation to see what would happen, Eve took the bait. Her eyes couldn't deny that the fruit was beautiful, and was good to eat. She believed Satan's lie that they wouldn't die and wanted the mysterious knowledge the fruit contained. Without fear, with one bite she played god in her life and then Adam played god in his and sin entered the world.

I am certain Satan, the Father of lies, celebrated his success as he thumbed his nose at God.

When we are ruled by unhealthy fear our reasoning is gone and Satan the great deceiver can draw us further from the one that gives us life and hope. But in this case, Satan cleverly removed the fear of death for Eve by contradicting God's words and motivation.

One must know that God sees everything and nothing can be hidden from his eyes.

The day of their reckoning came when God, knowing what they had done, walked into the garden. They couldn't escape Him or the fact that this chosen disobedience changed them forever as they were naked before God in every way. Knowing this, they hid themselves from their Creator.

Shame and fear will cause a person to do just that. Shame grows when we cross a God given boundary and we do things that we know are wrong. As a result shame walls are built that we use to hide behind in order to cope and can become an emotional prison if we stay there.

Fortunately, the prison door isn't locked. We can repent and step out of the shame right into God's loving arms. If we choose not to, the shame of disobedience can and will lead us away from Him in rebellion. There is no middle ground as these unrepentant behaviors will lead to spiritual death and separation from the goodness of God.

But sometimes we feel shame for other reasons. This can happen when we experience trauma and abuse through no fault of our own. Innocent and unprepared, we can fall victim to those followers of Satan who choose to do what is unspeakable.

What is important to remember is that God sees this too. He sees, He knows, and He cares for those who suffer this kind of harm.

This kind of injury also has a shame wall that includes fear, anger, secrets kept, and results in adaptive behaviors that come at a high price and can become an emotional prison as well, if we stay there.

But there is hope and we can step out of the shame right into God's loving arms and find peace.

Within the years of my life, Satan has continually sought to destroy me. First through the neglect of my parents, and when that could not be accomplished, He used my mother in an outright attempt at taking my life. When that attempt failed, Satan patiently sat ringside biding his time waiting for his next opportunity.

While still in my preteen years, Satan knocked on the door masquerading in the body and mind of one of my brothers.

I was still too young to understand that Satan is clever and can bring trouble to your door dressed in blue jeans, tennis shoes and a shirt. He can look innocent and be welcomed without a thought. At least that is how it started with a Christmas time visit.

The initial excitement of this older brother's wish for a Christmas visit and his arrival by train in Ardmore was wonderful. It had been many years since I had lived with my brother in my early childhood home and seeing my brother Tom for the first time since I was four years old felt strange. I had no early memory of him. He was three years older than I and was in grade school when I left my natural parent's home.

This Christmas holiday visit went well and we delighted in getting to know him after so many years apart. This short but pleasant stay ended and with no alarm bells ringing that would prevent his return, he asked to return for a visit during the summer months and our parents said yes.

That summer.... the summer of 1967, started off with the fun of our brother's return. It was filled with morning trips to the donut shop in town to satisfy our stomachs with the heavenly sweet, glazed donuts produced there.

The mornings were fun and as the days progressed all seemed great. We were enjoying the time we all spent together but this joy didn't last.

Unfortunately for me, during this time period, my parents, not being aware of the danger he represented and the need to protect me, placed him in the living room, next to my bedroom to sleep. At night, he would slip into my room to talk. Soon, he suggested that I should learn how to kiss boys by allowing him to kiss me. There was never any sexual penetration, but it was inappropriate, and sexual abuse.

Within days my brother's attention turned and focused solely on someone else and was unfortunate for them. The scars from this focused attention have wreaked havoc on the other person's life in a thousand different ways.

I don't know to this day how our parents discovered what our brother was doing but I'm thankful that after it was discovered they stopped any further abuse from taking place.

Unfortunately you can't un-ring a bell, the damage was already done, and has lasted a lifetime with scars that remain. There was my life before, then my life after, and it was never the same. How could it be?

When I look back at this event it's important to know that my parents never knew that what was happening to my brother's other victim was happening to me as well. I never told them.

There was so much turmoil as a result of what they already knew about and feeling shame over what had happened to me, I just couldn't open my mouth to tell and the construction of my shame wall began. I wanted to be free of the way I felt about it all.

When my brother left, we moved on as if nothing ever happened. Nothing to be done. Back to the day to day.

I was eleven years old and knew nothing about sexual abuse. I felt shame that my brother had taken advantage of my innocence and as often happens blamed myself. I know now I had nothing to blame myself for. I was a child.

The shame and anger over the sexual abuse I experienced stayed deep. Shame has it's own power that keeps secrets buried with a false sense of safety. But it is just that...false. It is a prison that prevents true peace and joy.

My shame wall kept these events buried for years even after I left home. But the shame continued to effect every aspect of my life. It was only after many years of marriage I felt safe in sharing this event with my husband.

When I had children of my own, the memory of my childhood event continued to feed the hidden anger and resentment I carried. With certainty, I would do anything and everything to protect my children from harm and I found it so maddening to think about just how unprotected I was. How could my parents trust someone I didn't even remember and they didn't even know?

I realize now that no matter what you do and the ways you train your children, harm can still come to them. Though we may try, not everything is in our total control. With this realization, I began to forgive the mistakes that my parents made in my childhood regarding this abuse but the relationship I had with my family continued to be troubled.

As a married adult, I still longed to feel love from my parents but time after time I would be rocked back to the reality of what their view of love looked like. Their kind of love continued to include verbal abuse, put downs, jokes about my body, and inappropriate comments to my husband about how he must view me sexually.

If anyone had questioned our parents asking do you love your daughters. They probably would have answered that yes they loved us. But...it felt like hate to me.

While I struggled with the relationship with my parents in my adult life, my longing for relationship with God grew and became lifesaving.

I am thankful that God is loving, kind, and patient with me because when things began to devastate me and I felt overwhelming shame that I wasn't worthy of being loved even by God, I would once again become afraid and try to wrestle the reins out of God's hands too. I would return to the wall of shame, hiding behind behaviors in an attempt to cope with the pain I felt.

It's common in human nature to want to avoid pain but that's not how God designed us and how we truly grow emotionally.

While I could avoid pain temporarily through addictive behaviors too numerous to mention, the medicated calm only lasted for a very short time. The pain I was trying to avoid would rear it's ugly head again, and the addictive cycle would repeat itself becoming a dead end road that produced nothing. This cycle named Addiction brought it's cousin, whose name was Guilt along for the ride and this combination worked against my attempts at emotional growth, leaving me prisoner once again.

But the truth remained...the prison doors were unlocked, I didn't have to stay there. I could open them, and if they seemed too heavy, I could ask for help because God was there with me. He lovingly provided the wisdom, insight, and strength that I needed which allowed me to open the heavy prison door of shame and set me free.

I grew to see with open eyes all of the ways He had held me in His hands. From the day I was born, God was shaping and molding me for His glory and purpose. Because He is loving and wise, He allowed the life struggle necessary to develop my character and build within me the strength and perseverance He desired. These attributes have given me help in times of great struggle and helped me to thrive.

In God's natural creation, even butterflies need to struggle to emerge from their cocoons to build the strength needed to enable their wings for flight. If in error you think you are helping and open up the cocoon for the butterfly, it will not survive.

In this regard, there is a gift within the struggle.

Sometimes it was hard to see my struggle as a gift and when things were too painful, I sought refuge within God's word. It was there that I discovered insight and am thankful for the early lessons and teaching found within it's pages.

One of the most impactful lessons for me came within my study of the historical account of Paul's journey to Athens and his interaction with the people living there.

Found in the New Testament book of Acts, I read the story of the apostle Paul who had traveled to Athens, Greece. He saw that the people of that Greek city had idols everywhere. One idol even had inscribed on it's base these words, " To An Unknown God".

These ancient Greeks certainly felt that there was someone greater than themselves. Their multitude of idols gave testimony to this fact and their worship of these man-made idols was evident. But, they were mistaken in their understanding of what God is like and with loving compassion Paul explained to them the nature of God.

I was no different than the people in Athens, Greece. I needed to know and understand what God was like too. I needed to dive into the Bible and see the goodness of God displayed on those ancient pages for the people of old who cried out to Him for help.

I needed to know that it was possible that God loved me and cared for me especially when I experienced moments of emotional pain. I needed to choose to see the past with different eyes; ones that were laser focused on what God had already done for me. These moments of awakened reflection have brought me peace.

God's love for me that is plainly seen in the present daily moments of my life continues to bring humility in my heart and praise to my lips. Each day is a gift and I know without a doubt just how much He loves me.

CHAPTER 10

MY CINDERELLA STORY

You are the God who
Performs miracles.

—Psalm 77: 14

certainly see God's love for me when he acted upon my behalf when I was fifteen years old. I had no idea this particular event was anything but an ordinary night in my life standing at a football game in Marietta, Oklahoma. But God is good and brought the stars in alignment for this once in a lifetime meeting; the night I met the love of my life and my very own prince.

There he stood with his best friend Larry who was talking to my sister. There were no fireworks like in the movies, no locking eyes across a crowded room, nothing at all but a quick introduction, and then it was over.

There was absolutely nothing about this meeting that was romantic or memorable because no fairy godmother had suddenly appeared to dress me in a beautiful ball gown with hair magically styled by her wand. There was no special carriage that was changed from it's prior pumpkin state and created to deliver me to the game. Instead, my magical carriage was a school bus, and even worse I was dressed in the most hideous 1960's style marching band uniform you've ever seen which included a hat on my head.

I soon discovered that there was indeed some magic in the night in spite of my band costume. Several weeks later this boy would tag-a-long with Larry on a trip to our home at Wirt so that Larry could spend time getting to know my sister.

Like it was yesterday, I remember my mother saying, "Get outside and be nice to that boy that Larry brought with him. Someday you are going to have a fifty year golden rolling pin with him." In translation, she was saying to me that someday, Kenneth and I would celebrate fifty years of marriage together.

When I think about it now, it is hard to wrap my head around the statement that she made. She had never claimed to be a prophet and if she had, I would've thought that she was crazy. I wasn't interested in going outside and talking to Kenneth Wiley. I already had a boyfriend and felt that doing so would be wrong, so I ignored my mother's wise request.

Before long my interest in the boyfriend I had at school began to quickly fade and it ended as young love often does. It was a short time after the end of that brief relationship that Kenneth began to return with Larry once more to our home at Wirt. He was three years older than I, was a Christian, and was more than cute. His heart was handsome, his face was handsome, and I became smitten. It wasn't puppy love this time.

I really liked Kenneth but after making several trips to my home to see me, he was discouraged from coming back by my sister and her boyfriend Larry. Due to their peer pressure and interference he began dating someone else and moved on. I was left heartbroken.

It was then I began to plead with God to allow me to marry Kenneth some day. Nightly prayers to God pled my case. After some time, with no hope in sight, I moved on too and dated other boys but Kenneth always held my heart.

Shortly before my seventeenth birthday I received news that Kenneth had joined the national guards and was sent to basic training. It had been two years since I had talked to Kenneth and when I received the news that he no longer was dating or seeing his girlfriend, my heart was filled with hope and excitement. I desperately wanted to write him.

While openly discussing plans with my mother to write to Kenneth while he was away at basic training, Wanda overheard me. Her expression of disgust and anger that I would write him filled the room as she angrily voiced her disapproval that I would even consider it.

But mother had always been my supporter where Kenneth was concerned and with God's help, mother hatched a plan to secretly deliver my letters to the post office. With clandestine activity worthy of a spy novel, I began to write to Kenneth while he was away and my secret agent mother delivered them to the post office.

My heart sang within me when I received his first letter in response. The letter was sweet with the promise from Kenneth that he would take me fishing when he returned home and my heart stayed hopeful that he would keep that promise.

The weeks dragged on waiting for his return home with letters sent and letters received between us that were filled with future plans and longing for him to be home again.

I will never forget the October night he called me after he returned home. I was so excited to hear his voice and hear him say, "Let's go on a date I'll pick you up Friday night!"

My opportunity to see Kenneth once more was filled with a mixture of hope and uncertainty. Would he be the boy I fell in love with still? How would he feel about me? So many questions remained to be answered and Friday night couldn't get there fast enough.

What a night it was! It was dark, it was raining, and we went to the drive-in movie. But to me, none of that mattered because the joy of being with him again was like sunshine. I didn't care about the rain. I didn't care about the movie. I only cared to know if his heart was free. We talked and talked because my heart was fragile and I bravely warned him, I couldn't take him breaking my heart again.

As the months passed we continued to date, love bloomed, and by February he wanted to buy me a promise ring but I said no. I didn't think my dad would approve so instead he bought me a necklace with his initials on it that I could wear and I was happy.

In the month of May I graduated from high school and was immediately sent off to attend summer college classes in Durant, Oklahoma. Kenneth was living in Durant that summer as well and was trying to catch up on the college classes he had missed by enlisting in the National Guards. That summer, Kenneth, my introverted, doesn't like attention, quiet with a strength I so admire man, proposed marriage one evening as we were sitting at the Sonic Drive-inn eating a hamburger. Still to this day he tells people I asked HIM. He loves to see my reaction but we both know the truth.

His question to me was, "Do you think your parents will mind if we get married in September instead of December?" With

September only a few short weeks away I wasn't about to let my hamburger or that question get cold. Without hesitation I said, "Yes, let's get married in September, my parents will not care."

Not long after I said yes, Kenneth went to my home to ask my dad for my hand in marriage. Thinking my dad would welcome Kenneth with open arms and a handshake, I was more than surprised by my dad's less than enthusiastic response. My dad said, "Well, I'm not paying for any divorce."

I loved Kenneth and wanted my dad and family to reply with kindness but instead, he was verbally splashed with ice cold water.

The great thing about Kenneth was that he wasn't going to let my dad's less than enthusiastic response bother him. He had made a commitment to me and he wouldn't let that go.

We also both knew that even though my dad's response wasn't loving or kind, it wasn't a definite no. Knowing that I would be eighteen soon and wouldn't need their legal consent, we carried on with our plans to marry and selected a date that placed our wedding a few days after my birthday.

The funny thing was that Kenneth was still weeks away from turning twenty one, the legal age for boys and his mom had to sign the papers for him when we applied for our marriage license.

After the summer college classes ended, the following short weeks were then filled with preparations for the wedding.

I was seventeen years old, young and clueless about all the many decisions that needed to be made. My poor mother!

Wanda and dad, took me to Wichita Falls, Texas, to find my wedding dress.

Kenneth's mother made our one of a kind wedding cake and after it was made, she said she would never make another like it. I wanted daisies on our wedding cake instead of roses and didn't realize just how much labor my choice required. My poor mother-in-law!

Five days after my eighteenth birthday, I said, "I do" at the altar to my prince while wearing magical Cinderella slippers. I have been wearing magical slippers ever since, and still to this day dance in the kitchen with my prince.

My dad's worry about our decision to marry has long passed but it hurts me to know that until the day my dad died, he never appreciated Kenneth, and always took every opportunity to remind him that he was second favorite of any man my sister was with.

These words, second favorite son-in-law, were verbally abusive and meant to cut. Kenneth never allowed those words to penetrate too deep, though years later he still talks about my dad saying this to him.

Kenneth, their son-in-law, has loved me and has been faithful to me our entire marriage. Kenneth, the selfless servant, in all the years he knew my family, and selfless in ways that were never truly appreciated and he wouldn't want known. Kenneth, who had never asked them for anything but my hand in marriage.

I praise God and thank Him for Kenneth. I praise God and thank Him for answering my prayers and for bringing Kenneth back into my life. As I write these words my mother's prediction has come true; Kenneth and I celebrated fifty wonderful years of marriage, September 8th, 2023.

I praise God that His timing was and is perfect. I praise God for answering my prayers.

Above all….. I know……God Is Good.

CHAPTER 11

GETTING A NAME CHANGE

Ask and it will be given to you;
Seek and you will find; knock
And the door will be
Opened for you.

—Luke 11: 9

My maiden name was Sarah Elizabeth Farthing. If you look up the meaning of the name Sarah, you will find that it means "princess," and if you look up the meaning of the name Elizabeth, you will find that it means "pledged to God."

In contrast the name Farthing is English in origin and literally means "one fourth of a pence or penny." A coin that holds very little value.

Names are given to children for so many reasons. They are proudly passed down from father to son, grandparent to grandchildren, and sometimes given to honor someone the family admires. Names are powerful things and the fact that I carried the last name of Farthing was nothing short of ironic.

Growing up I had children make fun of my name, mispronounce my name, and adults look down on me because of my name. Someone once even said my Farthing family and I were trash. But God's love has a way of changing things and it wasn't long before His love and care did just that.

I was very much in love with the man God had brought into my life and knowing you are truly loved by another human being is a powerful thing. It meant everything to me. Marriage to him had been a constant prayer and a dream for so long and with God's help, it had come true. With hope, love and great expectation Sarah Elizabeth Farthing became Sarah Elizabeth Wiley.

It is interesting to note that the name Wiley means, "resolute protection," and is Scottish in origin.

Along with my name change, something else changed as well. I had a new home, a new beginning and the timid hope that things would be different.

Yet into this marriage I carried all the past childhood heart-ache I could hold with the constant belief that at any moment someone who said they loved me would walk away without a thought or care. Trust would be hard for me to give even though I wanted to believe it could be different.

In our early months of marriage Kenneth never complained about my cooking or anything really. Kenneth always had an easy going nature and a great sense of humor. It has never been his nature to complain about anything and his sweet nature made our lives sweet and wonderful. He was patient, loving and kind. He never used his words to cause the kind of pain I had experienced growing up.

The first year of our marriage, we traveled home practically every weekend staying one night with his family and one of those nights with mine. To his credit, my husband was trying to finish his last year of college in Durant, Oklahoma, and at the same time was starving to death. He only survived on the weekend meals that were served by his mother and mine. I mean really… I couldn't cook.

One night, with zero experience in the kitchen, I tried to make a romantic "one month" anniversary meal. With a grocery store boxed spaghetti in hand that even included the can of sauce along with a small packet of Parmesan cheese, I thought, garlic bread would be great with this. I went to my cookbook and found there a recipe I thought was perfect and fixed that. Unfortunately, I made French toast. I thought, "This can't be right, when am I supposed to add the garlic?"

I truly knew nothing about food, how to cook or even obviously how to understand the difference between garlic bread and French toast in a cookbook. Romance turned to tears when Kenneth sat down to eat and asked for the pancake syrup. I ran from the table crying and locked myself in the bathroom. Poor guy, he never knew what hit him.

His love and patience with me was a gift and he is my hero for not dying from starvation during that first year with me.

As much as God is grieved over the actions that disappoint, I wonder if He was laughing in humor watching my attempts at cooking. I thank God He kept Kenneth alive in spite of the lack of my kitchen skills.

I also thank God for showing His great love and patience over me as I struggled with His recipe book to produce a life that would be pleasing to Him. As I came to realize after marriage, there is a difference between sitting and watching someone cook and the actual cooking of a meal and the knowledge that comes from that. No real cooking knowledge came for me until after the first year of my marriage.

Learning to cook is not a spectator sport. No amount of watching can compare to the actual work required, the gathering of the needed utensils, the gathering of the essential ingredients, getting your hands in the dough, and all the steps needed that bring about a meal. Even then, that is not enough. You can have all the ingredients, all the utensils, and all the knowledge but unless you do the work required to complete the process, nothing really is learned or produced of value.

Later in life after I left my childhood home, the same thing held true in living the Christian life that God desired for me. It wasn't a spectator sport to be observed from the kitchen bar stools or while sitting on the pews at Church. Observing others living their Christian lives as examples before me played a part, but I had to go beyond observing and get to the doing.

For me, in first learning to cook, a recipe book was necessary and helpful. In living the life that God desired for me, His recipe book was essential too.

There were other lessons learned in those early years of marriage too. I also got to see up-close, the difference in family dynamics and how Kenneth's family acted toward each other and how my family had interacted in my childhood home.

Kenneth's growing up years were a stark contrast to mine. His parents, Mary and Bill Wiley, raised their four children within a small modest home inside the city limits of Ardmore, Oklahoma.

Mary, a stay-at-home mom, decorated cakes for the community for extra income while wrangling three boys determined to terrorize their sister.

I have nothing but love and admiration for the woman Mary was. She was devoted to her family and God, loved on people in her community and I was grateful to be able to have the privilege of calling her Momma Wiley.

Bill, a veteran of World War II, was a man who loved God and country and most of all his family. When the war ended, he returned to Ardmore, Oklahoma to work at a Barber and Beauty Supply in town. He spent his days delivering beauty supplies to the shops in town and those out of town. At the same time he did the accounting for the beauty supply where he worked. This job, though not difficult for him, gave him a sweet relief from the scenes of war that I am certain haunted him.

To say his family knew who was in charge would be an understatement. The authority he held at home kept this family glued together in absolute unity with love for each other.

But, he had a soft side too. I will never forget the way he reacted in the moment he stepped into the room to see me in my wedding dress for the first time….he cried…it was so sweet. I was delighted to marry his son and be given the gift of calling him Papa Wiley.

There was no doubt these two parents were Godly people who loved and adored their children. There was no drug abuse or neglect or attempts to rid themselves of their responsibility by giving away of their children to strangers or verbal abuse. Their love for their children was demonstrated by their genuine interest in whatever their children were involved in, their desire for them to know about God by taking them to church, and the firm discipline that was meted out when needed.

Though their home was small, it was welcoming and full of laughter. The noise of their four children filled the rooms when they were all together and at times was explosive especially if they were watching a favorite football team on television.

Christmas under their tree while their children were young and growing up included one toy for each child, maybe a new pair of shoes or jeans, or an item needed for school. It wasn't extravagant.

The children within the Wiley's home were covered in a deep blanket of parental love that was spoken and unspoken. They knew without question that they were treasured and so loved. These children were never told how to feel about anything as their feelings of grateful, loving devotion were the natural result of the life they lived with their parents.

Kenneth's parents didn't keep reminding them they should be grateful for the things that they did for them. They never threatened them with abandonment. I'd never experienced anything like it. They not only seemed happy, they were happy. It was wonderful.

Seeing their example of family life helped me to realize that things could be different for me in the home that Kenneth and I created together. With God as the center of our lives and His word to guide us, I found the courage to believe and hope that Kenneth was actually someone who loved me though my insecurity and inability to believe I was capable of being loved continued to be an issue for some time. God and Kenneth's steadfast love showed me what love looks and feels like and both have been a stabilizing factor in my life.

Without a doubt, God's hand was all over the moment Kenneth and I met and I'm so thankful I now carry a different name.

CHAPTER 12

THE EARLY YEARS

And we know that in all things
Gods works for the good of
Those who love him, who have
Been called according to
His purpose

—Romans 8:28

The first nine months of our marriage was spent with Kenneth studying for his college classes, and teaching a college class. We entertained ourselves at night on a zero budget by watching Hogan's Hero's on television, doing puzzles, and each weekend we traveled to our parent's homes where great food was a certainty.

In the month of May, 1974, Kenneth completed his studies at Southeastern Oklahoma State College in Durant, Oklahoma, and received his bachelor's degree.

At the time, we thought we would be moving to Stillwater, Oklahoma, where Kenneth would study to obtain his Master's Degree in Computer Science while working for Oklahoma State University in an assistantship program they offered. But God had other plans and before that could happen, Kenneth received one amazing job offer that took us in the opposite direction to the Dallas, Texas, area to work for an oil company. Life seemed like an adventure and we both were so excited to see what the future held.

Kenneth began the grind of driving in the heavy traffic into downtown Dallas to work everyday and being young, it didn't yet weigh heavy on his spirit.

Most weekends living in the Dallas suburb of Carrollton, Texas, were spent with friends from church or relaxing at home but one weekend a month we would travel back to Oklahoma so that Kenneth could join his army national guard unit in Sulphur, Oklahoma, not far from Ardmore.

Three years quickly passed living in that small upstairs apartment in Carrollton with Kenneth driving Monday through Friday into work downtown in Dallas.

Though life was good living in the Dallas area and we were finding friends and enjoying our young married life, a painful event would occur that brought back feelings that would cause me deep insecurity and hurt.

During this time period I was molested a second time. When this event occurred it was devastating to me. I lost complete trust in my offender. It was never the same. I immediately told myself, just keep this to yourself and pretend this didn't happen.

For so many reasons, I just wanted to block this event out of my mind but secrets can kill. It was only a few years later after my children were born, this past event bubbled to the surface and I began to experience depression. Thoughts of not wanting to be alive raged within me accompanied by anxiety attacks.

Satan stood by in evil anticipation not yet totally satisfied as he continued to try to take my soul.

The worst part of victimization is that sometimes those closest to you who could or should be supportive may be unable to understand the gravity of the betrayal, might not believe you, or tragically abandon you in support of the one who has hurt you.

I have personally experienced and seen the lengths people will go to in an effort to protect a sexual offender in a family and those within the body of believers in Christ.

Because of proximity within a home or at church to someone who is a sexual offender, the one victimized continues to feel unsafe in their presence, and may seek support from others in the community of believers in Christ or within their own home. If not supported by their family or church body, the one victimized may, as a last resort, turn elsewhere for relief.

Under both circumstances of abuse that happened to me and occurred years apart, I, for a long, long, time chose to remain silent but this silence came at great personal cost to me and though I felt my silence prevented pain it only made the pain deepen. Inaccurate feelings of guilt and wondering what I did to cause this to happen to me were overwhelming and painful. This secret kept me ill and off balance and desperately needed the light of day.

Even though both offenders died a long time ago now, the scar of those wounds remain. Healed over, but not forgotten.

In homes everywhere, churches, work places, wherever people are, sexual abuse takes place and is perpetrated upon the innocent and unprepared. There are men offenders and women offenders alike. Offenders inside the body of Christ, and those outside. There are people from every walk of life you can name or imagine, that commit unwanted sexual acts upon others. It is pervasive in our society.

There is denial, there are secrets kept, there is fear, there is acting out. There is pain buried, pain not buried. But let me say... whether in this life justice is brought about through the legal justice system or the next, without repentance by the one who has committed this injustice, God's ultimate judgment waits. Nothing can be hidden from his sight.

He is the One who spoke the world into existence, He is all Powerful, He is all Knowing, all Good and Just, and God's promise of justice waits. He has seen, He knows about it, and He cares for those who are victims. In that knowledge, there can be the beginning of peace.

The thing that is hard for us, those of us injured by an offender and caught up in the anger and rage of an injustice done is that we may want immediate earthly justice. We might even want to be the ones who carry out vengeance in any way possible. When seeking justice through the court system the person that has harmed you may even be convicted and have to be incarcerated for their crime. We might receive justice in that way and rightly so.

But the other truth I want you to understand is that God's mercy extends to anyone who comes to him in repentance. Though that person may still have to live out the remainder of their lives incarcerated while on earth, when they turn to God determined to seek forgiveness, God is merciful and willing to forgive.

God is able to take all the sin, all the dirty secret stuff, and remove the stain of it, making the sinner white as snow. Only through His love for us is this possible and the death on the cross of Jesus Christ. Only with repentance, confession and obedience to Christ is there hope for all mankind.

> "Do not take revenge, my dear friends, but leave room for God's wrath, for it is written: "It is mine to avenge; I will repay," says the Lord."
> Romans 12: 19

> "Do not be overcome by evil, but overcome evil with good." Romans 12: 21

Without a doubt…God's love can heal and bring peace. My prayer for anyone suffering as a result of sexual abuse is that they can find comfort in the knowledge that they are not alone. I pray that God will send angels of comfort to bind your wounds and mend your heart.

CHAPTER 13

WHEN GOD SENDS ANGELS WITH SKIN ON

Sweet friendships refresh the
Soul and awaken out hearts with
Joy, for good friends are like the
Anointing oil that yields the fragrant
Incense of God's presence. So never
Give up on a friend or abandon a friend
Of your father....for in the day of your
Brokenness you won't have to run to
A relative for help.

—Proverbs 27: 9-10

Throughout my life God has provided people who are the embodiment of angels to soothe my wounded heart.

These souls, these angels with skin on, have blessed me with their kindness, compassion, generosity, and love. I can't imagine what my life would have been without them.

But friendship is more than a band-aid that is only needed for a short time. In the right hands it is a gift that can bring someone closer to God where healing of the soul takes place and a path in life that brings ultimate peace, hope and joy.

While I was still in my twenties, living in Carrollton, Texas I had a dear friend, the daughter of a gospel preacher, give me this advice. One day she said to me, "Always choose friends that make you better," and so I did. I stuck to her like glue and indeed, being friends with her made me a better person.

Throughout these many years our friendship has remained strong with conversations that have been meaningful, molding, and marriage saving. We've spent many cold winter nights bringing in the New Year and hot summer days celebrating July fourth watching fireworks while our children played nearby.

And then, there was the day not so terribly long ago that this same dear friend traveled over two hundred miles to bring comfort as she sat beside me, quietly holding my hand as I sat graveside mourning the loss of sweet Wilma, as she was laid to rest. That moment of grief, blanketed by her goodness and compassion, cannot be replaced and I cannot imagine my life without her in it.

Everyone needs someone like her, a true, deep, lifesaving friend who is the embodiment of an angel on earth that will hold you up through the storms life brings.

But sometimes, angels with skin on come disguised in the body of a young mother-to-be, living in another apartment across the street, and delivered by God right to your door. This meeting occurred a few weeks after we had settled into our apartment and new life in Texas.

After moving in to our small abode, things in the kitchen remained sadly the same as poor Kenneth continued to suffer through my offerings of boxed spaghetti and hot dogs without complaint. Only once a month, when we traveled back to Oklahoma, did he get any relief from the less than appetizing food I produced in that small apartment kitchen.

I still didn't know how to cook but I did have previous cooking expertise before marriage. My skills in the kitchen included the ability to open a can of corned beef hash, put it in a pan and heat it on the stove. My other kitchen triumphs included buttering soda crackers and toasting them under the broiler in the oven. I was gifted at making fried bologna sandwiches, and I hope you will try this, peanut butter slathered on white wonder bread with flaked coconut placed on top, then toasted under the broiler until the coconut is slightly browned and the peanut butter looks melted. See....I was amazing.

But Kenneth didn't like peanut butter, or corned beef hash. He never asked for crackers with butter slathered on them and toasted under the broiler and strangely...no television producers came calling for me to have a cooking show.

Again the Lord provided help in the form of a young expectant wife and neighbor that lived in an apartment complex near mine. She and her husband also worshiped at the same church we did. It wasn't long before we were great friends and I found out that this girl could cook! Hallelujah!

Like a child being fed something sweet for the first time, with eager anticipation for a second bite, I asked her for recipe after recipe so that I could delight my sweet husband at dinner time with something better than a hot dog.

From that moment on, I expanded my collection of recipes and put into practice the things I had learned. My usual underwhelming food offerings became a thing of the past and meal time was met with folks asking, "Can I have seconds?" My answer to that was… YES!

Have you ever contemplated requesting seconds from God? I do. Often my prayers have included this statement, "Please God, give me wisdom and insight," because I need more of both.

When I was young, in the early years of my marriage I wanted to be the kind of friend that had open arms with open doors to others… so I did.

In my later years, I wanted to be the kind of friend that would travel across the world if necessary to give life and hope…so I did.

I wanted to be the kind of friend that shares recipes and wisdom like my friend who cautioned me early on to choose friends that make you better…so I did.

You see, it isn't enough to want something. You have to step out of your comfort zone and behave yourself into change.

I am so glad I did.

CHAPTER 14

RETURNING TO THE ASHES

He will wipe away every tear from
Their eyes, and death shall be no more,
Neither shall there be mourning, nor
Crying, nor pain anymore, for the
Former things have passed away.

—Revelation 21: 4

I n the month of October, 1989, the news came to one of my brothers that our natural father had died and so we, his five children, gathered together to attend his funeral that was held in Vinita, Oklahoma.

It's hard to describe the feelings I had as we all sat on the back row of the packed Church during our father's funeral service. We sat there huddled together one more time unified as siblings. We, the not chosen, not wanted, abandoned remnants of a previous life.

As we sat there on the very last pew in the back of the Church, separate from the group of mourners sitting in the front family seats along with those gathered from the community to offer comfort, we were witness to love being poured out over a man we didn't even recognize.

This man was not the man we knew. We had lived with the drug addict, the man who, without a thought, had abandoned three of us, his own children, and had emotionally abandoned his two sons that remained in the home.

Though they remained in the home, these two brothers endured a childhood of abuse and neglect that affected them the rest of their lives. Their stories of abuse made my heart hurt. So… just who was this stranger they were talking about, whose body lay in the casket at the front of the Church?

Words of adoration, accolades, and admiration assaulted our ears while we remained at the back of the room, frozen in our seats.

Instead of grief for the loss of my father, I felt a combined sense of anger and pain. I can't describe how emotionally painful it was as I sat witness to all the love poured out by my father's community over his life. My angry heart screamed within me, where was this man so admired, this father, when I needed him, when we all needed him?

As the service for our father continued, the ironically acidic words of adoration, the accolades, the admiration pierced my heart like a thousand pin pricks and made my heart bleed profusely and for a long time after.

Determined to see things to the end, we then traveled together to Fort Gibson for the graveside ceremony.

No one looking on would have known the anger I carried to that graveside. It was extremely difficult for me to see these dead and living ghost of my past. The smoldering anger and pain within me grew into a flame as another event at the graveside service fed and fanned the flames.

Though I am sure it was meant to show us kindness, it didn't feel kind to me when a woman, who apparently had worked for my father, approached me to say how much our father loved us. I am sure she believed this, but I knew what she couldn't know about our lives. Her words were like kerosene on a smoldering fire and the anger within me raged and burned hot while she stood there unaware.

I find it interesting how our father could live a public life that looked wonderful but his private life was a living hell for the ones he lived with and gave birth to. His behavior wasn't loving and not what love looks and feels like.

I know only too well the effect and long term ramifications of this kind of "loving" treatment to those of us who experienced it. I know the feeling of abandonment and the lived out insecurities, the food addictions in attempt to not feel pain and anger, the drug addictions, the alcohol addictions, and sexual additions that my siblings struggled with and are a result of unhealed, deep seated, long term pain.

My father's death brought with it a silence and a finality but no closure to the wounds that remained unhealed in my heart. And so, the anger from those wounds continued to burn unable as yet to be quenched.

But long held anger and open wounds are destructive, and with one ghost of my past no longer living, I began to long to find my natural mother.

CHAPTER 15

A WISH COMES TRUE

Blessed are they that mourn:
For they shall be comforted.

—Matthew 5: 4

S tar light, star bright, first star I see tonight, wish I may, wish I might, have this wish I wish tonight. Have you ever heard this phrase or said it while gazing at the sky?

One day while traveling in the evening, looking through the car windows, the stars were shining so very bright. I began to think about the wishes we make in life and the sharing of the journey of my life, good and bad with others. Throughout my young adult life I wished to know what happened to my natural mother after she left us.

The irony of our abandonment is not lost on me, as she was abandoned by her mother as a child. It's hard to understand why the memories and pain of her own loss didn't keep her from repeating the pattern and with determination this behavioral pattern of abandoning children was broken and not repeated with me.

I have strong vivid moments and memories of my mother. Memories that are warm, loving and sweet. My earliest memory is one in which I am standing beside her in the kitchen drinking from a baby bottle. I can almost taste the sweetness of the milk I was drinking.

When I first came into the home at Wirt, I cried wanting my natural mother often. Later in my young adult life, I wondered each birthday if my mother remembered me or even thought about me at all. I will never know.

Two years following our natural father's death, I hoped to finally discover where our mother had gone when she left us so many years before. During the spring of 1991, with crazy determination, I became a detective fully invested in finding her.

I picked up my telephone and began my search, calling places where I knew she had been. People I talked to were kind and helpful and each one gave suggestions trying to help me find her.

Eventually someone during one of those calls suggested I could locate my mother through the board of nursing where she received her RN number. Knowing she had gotten her registered nursing license in the state of Tennessee, I made the call to the Tennessee Board of Nursing.

In hopeful anticipation I waited in my Oklahoma kitchen as the phone rang in Tennessee. The lady answering my call was kind and helpful and quickly found my mother's file. Within two weeks of searching, all my years of wondering were about to come to an end. But this ending wasn't joyful.

The lady on the phone told me with regret, that my mother's file contained a letter with information that my mother had passed away and had died in Bakersfield, California.

I never expected this kind of news and the knowledge of her death was devastating to me. So many questions remained. What happened and when did she die? Thankfully her file contained an obituary that detailed the news of her death and from there the rest of her story was told. After the end of her marriage to our dad, and abandoning her five children, she had remarried and then later adopted a baby girl. It truly broke my heart.

When this adopted child was six years old, my mother died. In the month of March, 1971, my mother abandoned all hope and committed suicide.

I don't know how many times through the years my mother had tried to kill herself. While I was still a child, I was told of a previous attempt years before in which her plan to shoot and kill me and herself was interrupted by my father. This time there was no interruption. No one stopping her. No one to say…we love you… No one to say…DO NOT DO THIS.

Learning this news was heartbreaking for me. I'd always hoped to find her.

Soon after learning of the death of our natural mother, my oldest brother Sonny and I, would journey together to locate and visit her grave in Bakersfield, California. Joining us there were my mother's sister, Margaret and her husband Phil.

Standing in stark contrast to the cemetery experience of our father, this journey was emotionally difficult for the four of us as we located an unmarked grave which was barren of any remembrance of her. As we, the ghost of her past stood graveside to witness and mark her loss, I felt an incredible sadness come over me. There were no words of love on a headstone, just a bare patch of grass with nothing to indicate her life mattered. Only two of her children willing to gather there to speak the words that she can no longer hear. Words spoken into the sky while tears fell onto my cheek, "I wish you could know how much we still love you."

My brother and I purchased a headstone for the grave there and engraved upon it the words, "We Never Forgot You."

I wish she could've known we loved her and love her still. I wish she could've known that she was more than her mistakes. I wish she could've known forgiveness expressed by others in love toward her and could've been able to forgive herself. I wish she could've known and felt the love of Christ. So many wishes remain.

You see, you can't erase your past, you can't bury it, and all the memories it contains. You can't leave behind five children and move on without emotional baggage dragging behind. I believe with all of my heart the weight of that baggage led to her death.

I pour forgiveness upon both of my parents. Their drug use, their neglect, and their abandonment of their responsibilities are forgiven by me.

I choose to let go of all the past except the lessons it has taught me. The trials of life have shaped my character and developed within me a compassion for others, healthy boundaries, and the willingness to forgive.

No matter what life brings I choose to lean on God when life feels too painful and when it doesn't.

Only one last wish remains for me. I wish to hear the words, "Well done" when I stand before my Lord and Savior, Jesus Christ.

CHAPTER 16

HEALING A BROKEN HEART

Trust in the Lord
With all of your heart
And lean not on your own
Understanding. In all of your
Ways acknowledge Him and
He will direct your path.

—Proverbs 3: 5,6

Have you ever wanted the emotional pain to stop? I know without a doubt I did.

When I was a young child, I was happy and felt loved by my parents and felt the relationship with my family was good. Things were easy and sweet.

But during my pre-teen and teen years, the adults within the family began to express their frustration and anger over the challenges of raising children that were not their own. With symbolic buyer's remorse, they began to regret their decision in bringing my sister and me into their home to raise. This led to angry outburst and things to be said and done by my family directed toward my sister and me that made my heart hurt.

In spite of their voiced regrets, as a preteen and teenager, my dependence on them would continue with the hope that they would somehow know that I loved them. I desperately needed to feel they loved me.

Once I was married my dependence on them ceased but my need for them to love me remained. It was then the relationship I had with my parents became even more difficult and strained as their thinking became twisted and distorted with the idea that my sister and I were fighting over what we would inherit from them someday. From then on, this crazy theme presented itself from time to time and I was viewed with suspicion.

The years of tightrope walking around them only became more difficult and at times, I completely fell off.

I was only eighteen when I married and left home, and too young to understand at the time that some troubles aren't quickly resolved and some relationships may never become healthy or healed. Therefore this strain continued for many years up until they died.

Family life for me wasn't like a television show in which all relationships are wrapped up in a pretty bow at the end, with smiles and joy. No amount of effort on my part could bring about relief and was completely compounded by a difficult if not impossible relationship with my sister.

No matter how much love I poured into both relationships, the one with my parents and the one with my sister in the hopes that it would change the way they viewed me and my relationship with them, things remained painful and the same. But like a lot of abused children, I kept on trying, going back to the source of the pain.

During these years, the feelings of pain and rejection built upon themselves into a torturous emotional weight that in time became unbearable and my feelings of frustration and self-hate displayed itself in my body and spirit. I gained a significant amount of weight and felt powerless to get control.

Episodes of binge eating became a vicious cycle. Self hate led to eating, and eating led to self hate. All of which numbed my mind and falsely placed a layer of protection for a broken heart and an unhealthy layer of fat around my waistline. All in a poor attempt on my part to cope with the painful experiences there at home and those thrown in by life in general.

Who knows how many times I joined Weight Watchers. That poor, sweet, weight watcher leader, probably felt like my first grade teacher, Mrs. Crisp, trying in vain to get me to go to the bathroom and not wet my pants, except in this case, dry pants were not the goal, but success for me with weight loss. Little did she know, the answer to my struggle couldn't and wouldn't be found there.

When my pain reached it's peak, I began to have the feeling that death would bring me relief but my love for my children and husband was strong and I was determined to not abandon them in this way. I wanted to live my life in a healthier way and in a way that gave my children a better example of how to cope when difficulty in life comes.

Sometimes friends can help us navigate when we cannot see which way to go. But sometimes, we need more than that in order to address the things that cause us to feel so low that death seems like an option. With resolve, I made the decision that I was going to stop trying to fix my pain without professional help.

There is a certain need for bravery when you go to get help. Bravery is needed to finally let go of the fear and pry open the doors of pain that have been buried deep. While bringing forth painful moments of life without anesthesia can be frightening, sometimes you just need to stop numbing yourself, allow yourself to feel the fear, and do what is needed to be healed and whole. This movement toward healing and uncovering pain for me was literally marriage saving and life saving.

The first ray of hope was found for me in the counseling office of a preacher in Oklahoma City, named Bill Smith. For approximately two years, on a weekly basis I would travel from Ardmore, Oklahoma to Oklahoma City where Bill's office was located within the church building where he preached.

I will be forever grateful to a sweet sister in Christ who kept my children while I traveled back and forth to get help. She will never know the life she saved in those years was mine.

Bill Smith was effective in opening up the layers of a covered over heart where the only thing I knew at the time was that I was depressed and couldn't figure out why. His first question to me was, " On a scale of one to ten, how do you think your parents giving you away affected you?" My answer to his question was zero.

At the time, this answer seemed totally rational to me but it was a prime example of how disconnected I was from the source of my inner turmoil and indeed there had been lots of turmoil, but any addict will tell you that turmoil can be quieted. I had become really good at quieting my inner anger and pain and putting other's needs above my own until I could do it no longer.

Over time, there in that Oklahoma City church building and preacher's office, my broken heart began to reveal itself and slowly the anger surfaced and I began the journey to healing. Bill Smith was so kind but was only able to take me part of the way on the journey. I will always be grateful to him for the ray of hope that started there within his office.

Dr. William Heitland, a professor and counselor in Ada, Oklahoma, then picked up where Bill Smith left off. It was there in his counseling office, the most help came. It was with his gentle guidance and skillful manner I was led to let go of the anger I had carried all my life, and then to the path of forgiveness directed over those who had hurt me. The first key to my healing was forgiveness. In the safety of this office....God provided.

Forgiveness, preached from the pulpit by various preachers for years, but unable to be accessed by me, began to penetrate my heart to the deepest layers within the walls of Dr. Heitland's office. The careful work on my heart began to surgically strip away the layers of pain that I had experienced throughout my life. This deep surgery also helped me to begin to recognize in truth there are no perfect people; not my natural parents, not the parents in whose home I was raised, not the sister I grew up with, not the friends I had, not my in laws, not my brother and sister-in-laws, not my husband and not my children. Most of all, I recognized, that I was a hot mess of imperfection and in that realization healing came. I finally and deeply understood that hanging on to the anger, self hate, hurt and disappointment was like staying in a self-imposed unlocked prison cell. I just needed to get out of my personal shame prison and step into the truth that the door was unlocked with God waiting on the other side ready to wrap me in His peace. If not, it would lead to my death. I chose and continue to choose life.

The second key to my healing focused on controlling my thoughts. I believe and have come to understand that my thoughts about what has happened in my life, matter the most because the way I chose to think could bring forth actions that would change my life, either for good or bad.

A great example of this is powerfully demonstrated in a movie called, "The Upside of Anger." In the movie, the main character, played by Joan Allen, believes her husband has deserted her. The result of this belief impacts her life in a negative way. She is so angry and has a distrust for men, not wanting anyone to get too close. Her behavior also has an impact on the two daughters she is raising.

At a crucial moment in the movie, men working and doing excavation on her property find her husband's body. Unbeknownst to her, her husband had taken a walk at the back of their property and had fallen into a hole and being unable to get out, he died there. She is devastated to realize that what she believed all along about her husband wasn't true. He had not deserted her. She had spent wasted years in anger and bitterness.

I sat in that movie and cried an ocean of tears. It was heart-breaking to watch this story play out. Why did this impact me so much? Because for years, I had told myself that no one could truly love me; not my natural parents, not my new family, not my husband, not my friends, and even worse....maybe not God. I had used every past experience in my life to support those thoughts. These painful thoughts and false beliefs plagued me and threatened to keep me prisoner.

Once more, I decided that freedom is not found without a fight. No special uniform was required for this battle, no boxing gloves, no weapon needed but COURAGE to step once more into a counseling office for more surgery without anesthesia.

It was there I gained the knowledge that gaining control of my thoughts could and would prevent disaster. I began to understand that how I thought was something that I could change and became a powerful tool in helping me to find joy and true peace.

This concept was explained to me in this very simple way using these initials.

E - Event

T - Thought

F - Feeling

R - Reaction

B - Behavior

C - Consequence

There is an event that takes place, this event creates a thought within you, the thought brings within you a feeling, the feeling brings a behavior, then the resulting behavior has consequences either good or bad.

I'd never had anyone explain to me that my thoughts were affecting my behaviors and I had the ability to change how I chose to think about things that had impacted my life. This seemingly small moment, like a pebble being thrown into a pond, had a huge ripple effect and was so helpful to me. It is interesting to note that this idea is not new. It is actually thousands of years old and one I had totally missed during many years of studying the Bible.

God had first shared the wisdom of controlling your thoughts, with one of the sons of Adam and Eve.

This historical account and the event surrounding it is found in the fourth chapter in the book of Genesis. It is the story of two brothers, Cain and Abel, the first two sons of Adam and Eve.

In the Biblical account we discover that Cain has a garden and grows crops while his brother Abel takes care of animals. One day they both bring offerings before God. Cain brings produce from his field, and Abel brings choice cuts of meat from his herd of animals.

Shortly after receiving these offerings, one son's offering is rejected and one son's offering is approved by God. This event sets into motion a teachable moment for one of these sons.

EVENT:

God has accepted an offering that Abel has brought before him. God rejects the offering brought before him by Abel's brother, Cain.

THOUGHT:

I don't know and can't know what Cain thought, because the Bible doesn't tell us. It could have been something like this......Why does God prefer my brother's offering? Why doesn't God like me? Abel, always the show off.

We can only guess. But no matter what Cain thought, I KNOW the feeling it brought about because the Bible tells us in Genesis chapter 4: vs 5

FEELING:

Cain was very angry, and his face was downcast.

How does God respond to Cain's anger? God in love for Cain gives him a warning and a caution.

> Genesis 4: 7
>
> "If you do what is right, will you not be accepted? But if you do not do what is right, sin is crouching at your door; it desires to have you, but you must rule over it."

REACTION AND BEHAVIOR:

Cain reacted to the anger he felt, ignored the warning from God, and killed his brother Abel.

CONSEQUENCE:

The first murder in human history; his brother Abel is now dead. This murderous behavior didn't go unnoticed by God because nothing can be hidden from Him. Cain is sent away from his family, his mother and father. He is punished because God would never allow the ground to produce food for him again. He is sentenced by God to be, " A restless wanderer on the earth."

Cain is marked in some way by God so that he can't be killed by anyone who finds him. The worst thing I believe and know within my heart, the worst punishment Cain received was his separation from God. Terrible… it was terrible.

Where along this timeline of events and this scenario could things have turned out differently? Where in this timeline was there an opportunity for change?

In response, most people believe the turning point would be with how Cain felt about the event. In truth the answer is not found there, but within what Cain thought about the event. God was cautioning Cain to get control of his thoughts.

Like Cain, I needed to get control of my thoughts because life for me had become full of moments of captivity and strongholds and looked like this: depression, food addiction, perfectionism, and a desperate need to control. It was exhausting.

Instead of asking God what he was trying to teach me, I spent my time trying to be my own god to make things work out because I desperately needed to be in control.

I hadn't been in control of anything in my life. I had no control of who my parents were, where I would go when their marriage ended, how I would be treated in my new home, and the sexual abuse that happened to me as a child or later.

I thank God for His loving kindness and patience with me because while still living out my captivity and struggling with my thought life, God was lovingly patient with me waiting for me to come home to Him.

I slowly began to understand I could choose how I thought about the events of my life. The events that caused me pain could either, through my thought choices lead me toward God or away from God. There was no middle ground.

This was a continual effort. Not a one and done deal. Practiced over a lifetime, and worked on, again and again. Necessary, so necessary for me as the relationship struggles with my family would continue for some time and the verbal abuse poured out by my dad upon me never stopped until the day he died.

Shortly before my dad's death, sitting in his chair in the nursing home, he said to me, " I hate you." Not sure I had heard him correctly I looked at him and said, "What did you say?" Again he repeated, "I hate you." In response, I looked at him and quietly said, "But daddy, I love you." That moment and memory still makes me sad.

The third key to my healing focused on developing a spirit of thankfulness.

This one-two punch of forgiveness coupled with thankfulness, slowly and gradually changed my wounded heart and became a powerful tool in healing from the emotional hurts I had carried for so long.

I began to express thankfulness in prayer to God for bringing people into my life at crucial moments. Thankful to God for the way He rescued me from death as He interrupted my natural mother's plan to kill me and herself years before. Thankful for the kindness shown me over and over through the years by God and the actions of love showered upon me by so many I believe are the embodiment of angels among us.

Thankful for the big things and the small. Thankful for the phone call from a friend that cheered my heart, the parking space close to the store, and even the love of a pet that greeted me with a wagging tail. Thankful for the beauty of nature in all it's glory and my ability to even see it. Thankful, thankful, gratitude to God.

The final key that was essential for me to find health physically and spiritually was the most important. It wasn't enough to have a forgiving heart. It wasn't enough to have a thankful heart. Though these were great attitudes to have, God expected a "doing" heart.

So I became a doer for no other reason than my love for God and everything He has done for me. As a result, this last action has taken me all over the world to share God's love for others and fulfill the purpose for which I was born. I pray the remaining years of my life are full to the brim with DOING.

In the years since the deaths of each member of the family that raised me, when driving by the home where I grew up, I still am overwhelmed by intense feelings and memories that can bring me to tears. I begin to feel the urge to eat in order to numb myself from the emotional pain I feel. But numbing myself is not the answer so if I feel sad and need to cry....I cry.

These trips home are infrequent now as the property that belonged to our family was sold and belongs to someone else. There is a beautiful young woman who owns it and resides there with her own dreams and a future that stretches in front of her that will be spent on the land. That fact makes me smile because she has wonderful plans and dreams to bless others.

But when I do go there, I never travel alone, because sitting beside me in the car is an angel with skin on that God has provided to bring peace, stability, and comfort to my heart while on earth; my sweet husband.

There is one more that travels with us. God is there, holding me in the palm of His mighty hand and I am thankful.

Get Up And Win The Race

Whenever I start to hang my head
In front of failure's face,
My downward fall is broken by
The memory of a race.
A children's race, young boys,
Young men; how I remember well,
Excitement sure, but also fear,
It wasn't hard to tell.
They all lined up so full of hope,
Each thought to win that race
Or tie for first, or if not that, at
Least take second place.
Their parents watched from off the side,
Each cheering for their son,
And each boy hoped to show
His folks that he would be the one.
The whistle blew and off they flew,
Like chariots of fire,
To win, to be the hero there,
Was each young boy's desire.
One boy in particular, whose
Dad was in the crowd,
Was running in the lead and
Thought "My dad will be so proud."
But as he speeded down the field
And crossed a shallow dip,
The little boy who thought he'd
Win, lost his step and slipped.
Trying hard to catch himself,
his arms flew everyplace,
and midst the laughter of the crowd
he fell flat on his face.
As he fell, his hope fell too;
he couldn't win it now.

Humiliated, he just wished.
to Disappear somehow.
But as he fell his dad stood up and
showed his anxious face,
which to the boy so clearly said,
"Get up and win that race!"
He quickly rose, no damage done,
behind a bit that's all,
and ran with all his mind and might
to make up for his fall.
So anxious to restore himself, to
catch up and to win,
His mind went faster than his legs.
He slipped and fell again.
He wished that he had quit before
with only one disgrace.
"I'm hopeless as a runner now, I shouldn't try
to race."
But through the laughing crowd
he searched and found his father's face
With a steady look that said again,
"Get up and win that race!"
So he jumped up to try again, ten yards behind
the last.
"If I'm to gain those yards," he
thought, "I've got to run real fast!"
Exceeding everything he had,
he regained eight, then ten....
But trying hard to catch the lead,
He slipped and fell again.
Defeat! He lay there silently. A
tear dropped from his eye.
"There's no sense running anymore!
Three strikes I'm out! Why try?
I've lost, so what's the use?" He
thought, "I'll live with my disgrace."

But then he thought about his dad,
who soon he'd have to face.
"Get up," an echo sounded low,
"You haven't lost at all, for all you
have to do to win is
rise each time you fall.
Get up!" The echo urged him on,
"Get up and take your place!
You were not meant for failure here!
Get up and win that race!"
So, up he rose to run once more,
refusing to forfeit,
And he resolved that win or lose,
at least he wouldn't quit.
So far behind the others's now,
the most he'd ever been,
still he gave it all he had and ran
like he could win.
Three times he'd fallen
stumbling three times he rose again.
Too far behind to hope to win,
he still ran to the end.
They cheered another boy who crossed the line
and won first place,
head high and proud and happy,
no falling, no disgrace.
But, when the fallen youngster
crossed the line, in last place,
the crowd gave him a greater cheer
for finishing the race.
And even though he came in last
with head bowed low, unproud,
you would have thought he'd won
the race, to listen to the crowd.
And to his dad he sadly said,
"I didn't do so well."

"To me you won," his father said.
"You rose each time you fell."
And now when things seem dark and bleak and
difficult to face, the
memory of that little boy helps
me in my own race.
For all of life is like that race,
with ups and downs and all.
And all you have to do to win
is rise each time you fall.
And when depression and despair
shout loudly in my face,
another voice within me says,
  "Get up and win that race!"

—Attributed to: Dr. D.H. Groberg

A WORD OF THANKS

This book would not have been written without the encouragement of my dear friend Barbara Taylor. It was during a lunch we spent together she suggested I should write my story. Thank you Barbara for the support and love you have poured over my heart during this process. I also want to thank my dear friend, Nancy Kymes for being my editor. Without her knowledge and experience the message within it's pages may have been lost. Most importantly, I thank God. He has blessed me beyond my ability to even comprehend. Until I draw my last breath, I will sing of the Goodness of God.